Book Endorsements

"As a psychotherapist, life coach and minister, Sherry Petro-Surdel has dedicated her life's work to helping people live their highest intentions. In *A Voice of Reason*, she brilliantly guides the reader on an inward journey of self-discovery through a series of inspired messages called Reasonings. Grouped into categories, each individual selection can also be examined on its own, perfect for personal meditation time or weekly book group discussion. Transformative and insightful, *A Voice of Reason* serves as an important book for all seekers of inner wisdom and spiritual growth."

~Salvatore Sapienza, author of *Mychal's Prayer and Gay as a Gift*, *ordained minister and workshop presenter*

"Sherry Petro-Surdel's spiritual journey, her wisdom, and her sensitive insights come shining through in her Reasonings. This is a thoughtful, inspiring book that will be invaluable to anyone on a spiritual path."

~Pamela Chappell, singer/songwriter, workshop presenter, minister and author of *For Pete's Sake*

D1444645

A Voice of Reason

Reason

Sherry Petro-Surdel

BALBOA.
PRESS

A DIVISION OF HAY HOUSE

University of Chicago Graduate Adler School of Professional Psychology Doctoral StudiesAcademy for Coaching Excellence Graduate Certified IMAGO therapist Ordained Universal faith minister

Scripture quotations marked (NLT) are taken from the Holy Bible, New Living Translation, copyright © 1996, 2004, 2007 by Tyndale House Foundation. Used by permission of Tyndale House Publishers, Inc., Carol Stream, Illinois 60188. All rights reserved.

All Bible references are from the King James Version of the Bible unless otherwise noted.

Balboa Press books may be ordered through booksellers or by contacting:

Balboa Press
A Division of Hay House
1663 Liberty Drive
Bloomington, IN 47403
www.balboapress.com
1-(877) 407-4847

Because of the dynamic nature of the Internet, any web addresses or links contained in this book may have changed since publication and may no longer be valid. The views expressed in this work are solely those of the author and do not necessarily reflect the views of the publisher, and the publisher hereby disclaims any responsibility for them.

The author of this book does not dispense medical advice or prescribe the use of any technique as a form of treatment for physical, emotional, or medical problems without the advice of a physician, either directly or indirectly. The intent of the author is only to offer information of a general nature to help you in your quest for emotional and spiritual well-being. In the event you use any of the information in this book for yourself, which is your constitutional right, the author and the publisher assume no responsibility for your actions.

Any people depicted in stock imagery provided by Thinkstock are models, and such images are being used for illustrative purposes only. Certain stock imagery © Thinkstock.

ISBN: 978-1-4525-7379-3 (sc)
ISBN: 978-1-4525-7381-6 (hc)
ISBN: 978-1-4525-7382-3 (e)

Library of Congress Control Number: 2013908087

Printed in the United States of America.

Balboa Press rev. date: 05/23/2013

Table of Contents

Sherry Petro-Surdel

Sherry is a gifted Life Coach and workshop presenter with over 25 years of experience inspiring and motivating individuals and groups to turn their dreams into reality. Her unique, soft spoken but success motivated style has made her a sought after keynote speaker and event presenter. *A Voice of Reason* is Sherry's first book.

Sherry's motto is that purpose and passion along with a plan, create success. Wishes are only wishes until there is a plan that works. Goals create successful plans. This is where Sherry's experience both in the world of psychology and coaching empowers others to succeed and reach fulfillment in ALL areas of their life.

Sherry's Mission and Purpose Statement: To be a contribution to this world by seeing all possibilities that assist others to live their highest intentions. We are here on purpose for purpose.

Sherry's keys to living a fulfilled life are Service, Integrity and Balance. She supports bringing out the best in others by bringing these components to everything she does.

<u>Qualifications and Education:</u>

- University of Chicago Graduate
- Adler School of Professional Psychology Doctoral Studies
- Academy for Coaching Excellence Graduate
- Certified IMAGO therapist
- Ordained Universal faith minister

Affiliations/Membership:

- National Association of Social Workers
- International Federation of Coaches
- Association of Humanist Psychologists
- American Psychology Association

Sherry has life coaching and counseling practices in Michigan and Illinois and is currently the pastor at Spirit Space, a Spiritual Enrichment Center in Saugatuck, MI.

Introduction

How It All Began

Quite a few years ago I found myself questioning everything I had been taught about religion, faith, God, relationships, the purpose and meaning of my own existence and other small details about the planet. As a result, I began a soul searching, life changing journey. I decided I had to visit and question most every belief I had held onto so tightly. I was determined to release anything that did not serve me or others well. I would write my own policy manual for my life. I never gave it a thought that this process would ever have much value for anyone other than me. Yet the truth is that everything we do, say and think does have an effect on something or someone. *A Voice of Reason* is proof of that!

Because I began this adventure; it has changed my life and I have been told, the lives of others. The adventure started 25 years ago. I had just graduated from a prestigious graduate school, with a clinical social work degree. I started a private practice and ended a 25 year marriage. I was scared and filled with excitement about what would be ahead. I was filled with questions. All of my life there was a yearning, an energy that moved through me that could not be explained. This energy created a deep interest within me in people and all things spiritual. I remember my uncle saying of me "She would debate Jesus Christ if he were standing here."

What I knew at this moment in my life was that this energy was running on such high voltage. It was the energy of what was true for me. I read anything that I could that applied to the infinite possibilities of spirituality, relationships, religion, psychology, philosophy and healing. This content would help me create my policy manual for life.

I was intrigued with anyone or anything that had even a remote possibility of opening up a window of understanding about who I was, who others are and who God is. I have found these to be pertinent questions for everyone to answer.

I needed to find the beliefs that were mine. I created my personal statistics class. In statistics class, for something to be statistically significant it must pass a reliability and validity standard. I would be the one to determine that standard. During this personal "stats" class, I entered a doctoral program, studied N.L.P. (Neuro-Linguistic Programming) and became a Certified Life Coach. This gave me valuable tools to shine a conscious flash light brightly on some of my most powerful conscious and unconscious belief systems (which I fondly call B.S.).

What I discovered and continue to uncover is that all of our answers are within us. I found a loving, non-judgmental Creator, an infinite source of wisdom to guide me and comfort me to co-create new possibilities. This Source supported me to be the best version of the highest vision I had ever had about myself, others and God.

I also found many wonderful guides, teachers and angels to light my way when the batteries in my conscious shining flash light started to run out of juice. I have been blessed with two wise old souls for children. They have taught me much about love, dignity, integrity and passionate living. You will see some of their wisdom running through the pages of *A Voice of Reason*.

To my son Clinton, I acknowledge the many conversations and the books shared about spirituality in all forms. His insight and foresight has been a light unto my path.

To my daughter Angel, you were named because you were the Angel in my young life. You are now an angel to the world of furry angels who need a nurturing, strong and benevolent care giver. Both of my children live a life filled with passion and personal integrity that does not hold to the standard of others but does hold to a true conviction from within.

To my dear friend Kathy. If it were not for her persistence and belief in making this book happen there would be no *Voice of Reason*. She believed in me and my journey so much that she made it her journey to see these Reasonings in print. Often we need someone in our lives that believe in our dreams even more than we do. One can never have a dream too big for reality is the gift that Kathy gave.

If all of this were not enough, I was also given a husband who encouraged me to do what my heart called me to do even when it made little sense to him.

What you are about to read began in my heart and then found its way to hand written words placed on three ring note book paper. These words were often spoken to a small group of seekers who gathered together to form a spiritual community called Spirit Space. The thoughts that turned into the spoken word are called Reasonings. Churches often call it sermons or messages. I call them Reasonings in reference to a biblical passage in Isaiah 1:18 which says, "Come now, and let us reason together, saith the Lord." This infers to me that it is a co-creation experience. I also appreciate the Rasta spiritual perspective which calls this co-creation process

Reasonings to understand (or as Rastafarians say to overstand) the ways of God.

Spirit Space is mentioned often in this book. Spirit Space is much more than a physical location. It is an energy that breathes in every one of us. It is that place within us that holds us when we are frightened, calms our anxiety and soothes us when nothing humanly can.

Spirit Space is the realization that we are all more alike than different and that we are an amazing creation filled with wonder and awe. Spirit Space is the place we dance with abandonment and partake in the fruits of our labor. It is where there is love, laughter and a sacred altar that displays the symbols of all that we hold dearly. Family, friends, our furry and feathered friends, our memories all set on that altar. It comes from experience, hard work, dedication, sacrifice and a desire to seek the unknown.

Spirit Space is also a physical location placed in the twin communities of Saugatuck and Douglas, Michigan. It is a place where weddings, births and deaths are honored and celebrated. It is our physical spiritual home. It is filled with those who give until there is no more to give. It has a meditation room with an altar that represents symbols of the major faiths of the world. The light streams in from the windows in all of its different shades, just as light streams out of our hearts in so many different hues and shades. There is always light and often shadows.

Spirit Space has much to learn, much to repair and much to give back. This is remarkably similar to everyone's personal journey. The Spirit Space mission statement says so much, "We are a spiritual community that reaches in to reach out."

The Reasonings found in this book came from my heart. They are given to me through the life that I have, people that I love and experiences that show up to help my soul evolve.

Before you begin to read *A Voice of Reason*, I offer this prayer. This prayer was created to celebrate the creation of our physical location. It is also a prayer for the Spirit Space within each of us.

From My Heart,
Sherry

Affirmative Prayer for Spirit Space

May the doors of Spirit Space be wide enough to receive all who hunger for love and peace, all who are lonely for friendship and care.

May it welcome all who have cares to unburden, gratitudes to express, hopes and dreams to nurture.

May it encourage one another to ask the tough questions so that we may grow individually and as a spiritual community.

May the doors of Spirit Space be so narrow that they shut out pettiness, pride, envy and prejudice.

May its threshold be no stumbling block to the young, to the truth seekers and the curious.

May the doors be too high to succumb to complacency, mediocrity, selfishness and harshness.

May this place called Spirit Space be a home for all who enter, seeking a more meaningful life. A place to go deep within and then offer opportunities to contribute to planet Earth and all living beings.

May our hearts be as open as our doors.

This is my dream,
Sherry

Dedication

This book is dedicated to Jackie McGhehey-Breault
(October 27, 1941-April 3, 2011)

She believed in infinite possibilities.

She believed in Spirit Space.

She believed in me.

She will always be in my heart.

Thank you Jackie for your foresight and generosity. You are missed but never missing. I feel your presence at Spirit Space as you promised I would.

Section I

Success and Purpose

Success and Purpose Introduction

One of my mantras is "We are all here on purpose for purpose." That statement best describes what will be found in this section of Reasonings. My master coach Maria Nemeth, founder of the Academy of Coaching Excellence taught me that to get where I want to go, I need to know <u>where</u> I want to be.

You all have been invited to the grandest party of the Cosmos, but you must respond to the R.S.V.P. You have already shown you are intrigued enough to open this invitation. See you at the party! It is where you are called to be.

Help, I Need a Policy Manual

Have you ever felt clueless about where to go next, or what to do in a particular situation? An example of that type of thinking would be: "I know others must have gotten something I didn't when wisdom was being passed out." Have you ever experienced this type of feeling? Have you ever asked God, "Where is my Policy Manual?"

Quite a few years ago I was asking myself some of those questions. There were decisions I had to make about my life. I needed to make choices about my future. I had been involved in organized religion for years. My mom had passed away the previous year and I wasn't sure what role I was to play in life. I began to think more deeply about the things that had worked for me (or should I say, I thought had worked for me). But everything just seemed to be leading me in circles made of brick walls and it seemed I was making some poor choices. Most of all I realized that for much of my life I had flown by the seat of my emotions. I also realized that I made many choices that were more about what I felt others needed or wanted than what I wanted. My motto seemed to be "How Can I Please You?" I was not focused on myself or God. God was always a central part of my life but I made it more of a one sided relationship. I was not sure what I needed to create my spiritual journey. I was looking to add meaning to my life and find my way. I tried to let God lead but it seemed the situations and my emotional state had the lead. I had decisions to make and I was looking for clarity confidence and divine guidance.

Remember, I did not get my Policy Manual.

I had left organized religion some eight years prior. I was done with the "religious community" telling me how to think, how to dress, how to raise my children, whether I could get a divorce, how to pray, and how to worship. They gave me their policy manual and said it was God's. I had to put this approach in my past. It just did not work for me.

I thought I'll have to figure this out on my own, because things were not all that great when I let others do it for me. I needed to write my own Policy Manual, create my own religion if you will. So my wilderness experience began. I did not realize it at the time but that was what Moses did when in the wilderness. He left his people and went to the place of the Burning Bush and received the Ten Commandments. He got his Policy Manual! It was something concrete (pardon the pun), something solid that he could use to lead the Israelites.

At Spirit Space we started out wandering around the dessert looking for our Policy Manual. We wanted something that would reflect the oneness, yet honor the uniqueness of us all. Something that will give us a clearer direction, particularly when decisions need to be made. This Policy Manual helps us to not fly by the seat of emotions, or wander for years in the wilderness, grumbling and complaining like the Israelites. And it is something that can be changed as we change. It must grow as we grow. There must always be flexibility and a willingness to surrender to all possibilities. It is no different in our own personal journey. We all need a policy manual that reflects who we are and provides clear direction.

Even rebels, free-thinkers, non-denominational, inter-faith, New Thought and "I'll do it my way" people need some direction and a Policy Manual.

We embarked on a Spiritual journey here at Spirit Space to create a worship and spiritual enrichment center that would give our spirit the space it needed to grow. Spirit Space is also the metaphor for your journey. We are creating something and it has not just been handed to us as a creed like other organized religions. We are creating and updating it. Just as in my introduction, remember there is a Spirit Space within each of us as well as a physical location. You are embarking on your own spiritual journey. You are ready to give birth where your inner sanctuary can grow your spirit.

Religion's purpose has sometimes been used to control a society, to support a cause, to dictate morality or to be used for a social meeting. Swami Yogananda said, "Self-realization is the true purpose of religion." It is to cause us to ask the following question, "Why do I exist and what is my relationship to the infinite universe that surrounds us?"

What is the purpose of an organized set of beliefs called religion for you? It is a good idea to update and validate your belief system from time to time.

As much as I baulk at being placed in a mold, I know a mold is sometimes necessary for success. Moses got the Ten Commandments. Jesus gave the Sermon on the Mount. Buddha the Dhammapada.

The Koran, the Bhagavad gita, The Dao, the Ching. All faiths have Policy Manuals, right?

Back to my story:

While wandering in my desert to find my own religion I realized I needed a Policy Manual that applied to me, personally put together by God, something that worked for me. I also realized for it to be successful, I must seek out the wisdom of the Wise Ones of the Ages. I created what I call the 357 Plan. It became my religion. I teach this content in a workshop for many of my coaching clients. I have a group of Spiritual Sisters that practice it and have for more than ten years. When Clint (my son) had the accident that threatened his sight and his life, I had to create a part two to be added to the original plan. It is called the Eliminate Emotional Suffering Manual. It also became a workshop.

My Policy Manual for my life is called 357. Three stands for the three words I choose each day that set my intentions for the Day. The words come from the following list of 26 words:

Authentic, Benevolent, Calm, Dauntless, Energized, Faithful, Grateful, Healthy, Inspired, Joyful, Kind, Loving, Mindful, Nurturing, Overflowing, Peaceful, Quiet, Renewed, Serene, Teachable, Unified, Vulnerable, Willing, XN (Greek letters for Christos), Yearning and Zestful.

I want to acknowledge Maria Nemeth and her coaching for the foundation of this idea.

Five is a reminder of my most cherished integrities. It is who I really am when I am operating from my highest. Mine are: Spiritual, Inspired, Compassionate, Generous and Courageous. Whenever I forget or get frightened, I remind myself or ask one of my Spiritual sisters to remind me of who I really am and they always do. In my workshop I teach students how to find their five major integrities.

Seven is the Seven Spiritual Truths. During my wilderness experience, looking for my Policy Manual, I realized for something to be TRUTH with a Big T (ultimate spiritual truth) it could not be just truth for one faith or culture, it needed to be truth for and from all religions.

I began searching ancient scripture and speaking to those of other faiths to find the thread that was the same, woven through all the major faiths to make the tapestry of truth for my life. I came to realize one would not even need to subscribe to a belief of any kind and these principles were still true and worked. Recently at Spirit Space I asked the trick question "Was our country founded on Christian Principles?" It was trick because it was founded on faith principles. America or Christianity does not have a patent on those principles. In my policy manual I provide Christian quotes, but each of these has a base in all other major faiths. A great example of this is: "Treat others the way you wish to be treated." In the book of Islam, Traditions chapter, "No one of you is a believer until he loves his brother what he loves for himself." And in Hinduism, "This is the sum duty, do nothing to others which if done to you would cause pain."

I came up with Seven Spiritual Truths that can found in some form in all the major religions of the world. They are as follows:

1. Treat others with the respect and treatment we want to receive.
2. We reap what we sow.
3. Two wrongs don't make a right.
4. Forgiveness is not an option.
5. A grateful generous spirit guarantees greatness.
6. What you think will determine your destiny.
7. Peace comes from God.

357—My Policy Manual for Life

Most days I create the intention for my day by consciously choosing three words to remind myself of my five integrities. These words also shine a conscious light on the seven spiritual truths. As things come up during the day that could cause me to question what is right for me, I call upon 357 to give me guidance and wisdom. At the end of the day I take time for introspection and examination as to how I demonstrated the 357 principles.

Having my Policy Manual that is based on universal Spiritual Truths has positively influenced my life in the last ten years. My motto is no longer how can I please you, but how can I support you and how can I serve my God? It has not only has changed my life but also has changed many others who have incorporated these principles into their lives. One day I hope to write a book dedicated to the stories others have shared with me about how 357 has worked for them.

Do you have a clear vision and mission statement for your life? Do you have a plan that will guarantee success? As I say about 357, "If you do it, it will work, if you don't, it won't."

If you are finding yourself wandering in the wilderness, maybe it is because you are looking for your Policy Manual. Remember only you and Spirit can create it.

Reasons to Go Within—Personal Application

Coaching Questions:

Take time to create a Mission Statement for your life. It is a great beginning to creating your own set of beliefs for your policy manual.

1. What do you want your mission statement to say?
2. How would having a policy manual in your life help you during those "wandering in the wilderness" times?
3. Knowing who you are when you are operating at your very best is what personal integrity is. What are some of your very best qualities?
4. What would you want to include in your policy manual for life?

Meditation:

Being gentle with yourself, breathing gently, honoring your amazing body, say thank you. Now honor your brilliant mind. From this mind you and God co-create great things. You and God are the co-creators of your life. God says, "I have great plans for you, plans for you to prosper in all ways."

Imagine if you will you and God creating a plan that will guide you through the maze of life. When you need some direction or clarity, there it is. This master plan has been woven from infinite wisdom and has been placed within you. When you need clarity, it comes. When you need direction it comes. When you need answers to your questions they are there, all within.

And so it is.

What Agreements Have You Made

Many are familiar with *The Four Agreements* by Don Miguel Ruiz. Oops, that was an assumption, wasn't it? One of the Four Agreements is to Avoid Assumptions.

I will not make that assumption. I will share with you a story of an ancient people who had a fascinating and extremely profound tradition. The people were given the name Toltecs by the Aztecs and this means Artist. As far as archeologists can figure, the Toltecs were not a race but a society of people found in Central Mexico. It is believed this society dates as far back as 200 BC. One could call them Spiritual Artists. Their tradition is sometimes called a warrior's path to Personal Freedom.

The greatest war we will ever engage in is the war within ourselves. We war with the limiting belief systems I fondly call B.S. We war with the domestication process and religious and cultural dogma versus the freedom to express our true nature. We sometimes fight the Divine Nature of God.

The most formable foes in our lives are the contracts or agreements we have made with ourselves that do not match who we are! These are contracts that do not serve us well.

Some believe that even before we are born we make sacred contracts. We then come to this earth to fulfill them. The distractions of this world create many challenges for us.

For you see these sacred contracts become hidden deep in our soul. Part of our journey here is to uncover them. It is thought that our sacred contracts become clearer as we live our passions and become a student of our own Spirit. Again sacred contracts are not always conscious. They are always NOBLE. That is where it becomes very important to be aware of the conscious agreements or contracts we are making with ourselves. I like to call it our Conscious, Sacred Path.

The Four Agreements as presented by Don Miguel Ruiz is a way of living that frees us from all the Agreements that are not the Truth but are part of our domestication. Children believe what they are taught and unfortunately much of what we were taught was not the Truth!

The Four Agreements frees us to live and find our Truth and to honor our sacred personal contracts. Don Miguel Ruiz was born into a family of healers. His mother was a healer and his grandfather was a shaman of the Toltec Tradition. Originally Don Miguel Ruiz began a career in modern medicine choosing not to continue in the century's old legacy of his heritage. After a near death experience, he returned to the tradition of this ancient wisdom. There is much to the teachings of Ruiz. Let us look at the Four Agreements from a biblical context.

Agreement #1—Be impeccable with your word

"The Spirit of the Lord spoke to me and its word was in my tongue." II Samuel 23:2

"Let you remain in me and my words remain in you. Ask then whatever you wish and it will be given you." John15:7

"May the words of my mouth and the meditation of my heart be pleasing in your sight, O Lord, My Rock, and My Redeemer." Psalms 19:4

In the book *The Four Agreements*, be impeccable with your word is considered the most important of the agreements. Your words have the power to create or destroy. Your intentions are demonstrated through your words. Impeccability of the word can lead to personal freedom, success and abundance. Don Miguel Ruiz suggests that you can attain the Kingdom of God, which is within us, by keeping this agreement.

We must avoid using our words to speak against ourselves and others. Our lives are abundant when we use the power of our words in the direction of Truth and Love.

Before you say something about yourself or others—Ask, Is that the TRUTH?

Your word is the power that you have created. It is a gift that comes directly from God—our creator. The human mind is like a fertile ground where seeds are continually being planted. When you are not impeccable with your word, your mind is no longer fertile ground, for the words then come from FEAR. What you plant and tend to will grow.

Impeccability of the word can be measured by your level of self-love. If you LOVE yourself, you will express that LOVE in your interactions with others. And that action will produce a like reaction.

What does it mean to be impeccable with your word? A word study suggests the word impeccable means without sin. Sin is not a word we use at Spirit Space. Sin just means missing the mark. It is an archery term. When you shoot an arrow and do not hit the center, you have missed the mark. So missing the mark is anything you do against yourself or another. It is not honoring who you really are and remember you are God's Perfect Child. Sin means separation from your own divinity.

Impeccability is of course telling the truth and doing what you say you will do. What you do to others, you are doing to yourself. We must eliminate the gossiping or slandering of another person. I believe it is in the spirit of keeping our word that is the Kingdom of God. The Spirit of Love for ourselves and others.

Do you keep your word to yourself? Do you speak words of love and truth to yourself? What contract have you made with yourself regarding your words?

Agreement #2—Don't take anything personally

"When I was a child, I spoke as a child, I understood as a child. I thought as a child. But when I became an adult, I put away childish things. For now I see through a glass darkly, but then face to face: now I know in part: but then shall I know even as also I am known." I Corinthians 13:12

Children are ego-centric and that means they believe <u>everything</u> is about them. That is why they can run into a room and interrupt without a second thought, and then be very confused when grownups say "Wait until I am finished." Children believe everything good that happens is about them and also everything that is bad is about them. This continues until they pass through the developmental stages that teach them a different truth. Many times we adults act as a child—We take things personally that are NOT about us at all. Many have gotten stuck in developmental stages that keep them childish. When this occurs life and people often seem more hurtful. Remember, the world is a mirror, what looks in, looks out. This agreement is a paradox. Everything is about you. Nothing is about you. A paradox is an assertion that may appear contradictory, yet is true. Don Miguel Ruiz says that if you honor this agreement, most of your needless suffering will cease!

Everything is about us. "We do not see things as they are, we see them as we are." Anais Nin

We each see and feel from our own reality. This reality is based on our history. No one else's reality has your unique history. Your opinions and point of view refer to your own agreements and are personal to you. Just as you interpret things from your reality, so will others.

Others are going to have their own opinion based on their belief system, it is not about you. Even when they say or think it is about you, it is still about them!

Remember that even the opinions you have about yourself are not necessarily true. Therefore, do not always take what you hear in your head personally. Do not believe everything you think.

You are not responsible for the words and actions of others. But you are responsible for <u>you</u>. Everything is about you because all that comes our way is here to help us grow beyond the self-imposed limits and belief system. This is part of our sacred contract. Additionally there is the idea of oneness. If it is a part of you, it is a part of another because via Divine Mind we are one. So when we hurt another we are hurting our self. It has been said that taking things personally is the maximum expression of personal importance or ego centric thinking because we make an assumption that everything is about us—just like a child.

Speaking of assumptions, that is agreement number three.

Agreement #3—Don't make assumptions

"And you shall know the TRUTH and the TRUTH will set you Free!"
John 8:32

One of the biggest problems with assumptions is we come to believe they are the TRUTH. The best way to stop yourself from making assumptions is to ask questions, collect data and assume nothing. Look at people and things with a healthy wonderment and curiosity, with unlimited possibilities.

The biggest assumption that we can make is to assume that everyone sees life the way we do and that everyone thinks the way we do. Therefore we think people should just know what we want or how we feel. We get wounded because they don't.

Don Miguel Ruiz says all the sadness and drama you have lived in your life is rooted in making assumptions and taking things personally. We must have courage to ask for what we want and we must not assume others should know. We need to accept that others have the right to say no and when this occurs, do not take it personally.

Highest love is accepting other people without trying to change them into our likeness. It is much healthier to be with someone when you already like who they are, then to try to change them into someone that you think you will like. When we stop making assumptions, our world becomes impeccable and our lives are transformed. Can you imagine how much suffering you have participated in because of making assumptions?

When you make assumptions, you gather evidence to prove it is true. We always get what we look for! A great example is a criminal evidence class I took in undergrad school. I was taught to never go into the crime scene with an assumption that I <u>knew</u> who did it or what happened. Don't accept something as TRUTH without proof!! This will rob us of our curiosity and wonderment. It will also blind us to the facts. What contracts have you made with yourself that are made up from the stories you have told or have been told? What is TRUE?

The Fourth Agreement—Always do your best

"I can do all things through Christ which strengthen me." Philippians 4:13

We are not required to do any more than OUR BEST. Remember your best is not going to be the same every day or every moment of your life. Your best is not overdoing. I tend to be an over doer, just in case it is not apparent to all those who know me. My son recently reminded me of this by saying "Just because you can does not mean you should." We sometimes decide on how much to do based on how much we can accomplish. This can cause a depletion of your energy supply.

By doing your best again and again, you can master the art of transformation.

I received a plaque for my birthday that says "I've learned that the Lord didn't do it all in one day and neither can I." If you do too much or too little you will experience frustration, resignation and cynicism.

Think about the following Chinese proverb, "If you chase two rabbits, both will escape." So remember to accomplish more is to focus on less.

From Aristotle, "Excellence is not an act, it is a habit."

To live fully in this moment, which is living your best, it is important to honor yourself with commitment. If you want to love what you do, do what you love and do it with your whole being. Let go of the past and enjoy the dream that you are living NOW!

Here are some tools for transformation:

>**Intention**—make a commitment to change the agreements that do not honor you or others

>**Attention**—Tame your monkey mind

>**Action**—Take action. Without action there will be no change—The word attraction ends with action.

>**Repetition**—Practice and practice until the new agreement is firmly established

We are not only to be seekers of truth but we must also be practitioners of the principles. The Four Agreements are great principles to practice! They will help you become conscious of your TRUE sacred contracts. Live these principles and you will live your sacred contract. If you enjoyed this Reasoning, I highly recommend that you read *The Four Agreements* by Don Miguel Ruiz. I read this wonderful book at least once a year. I do my best to practice these agreements on a daily basis.

Reasons to Go Within—Personal Application

Coaching Questions:

1. What are contracts you have made with yourself that don't serve you well? (Please remember to go within and see if it is something someone else has told you about yourself and you believed it.)
2. What new contracts would you like to make with yourself that will serve you well?
3. How can you apply the statement, "Just because you can do something doesn't mean you should"? Can you see how this belief system can deplete you of energy and cause you to lose focus of your passions?

Meditation—The Four Agreements

Go to your safe place. Know that where you are, all is well. Remember to breathe comfortably and slowly. Pick one of the agreements and repeat it to yourself three times. Now imagine that your spirit and body are one, no beginning, no end. You are the essence of being before you ever were. You and the Divine are not on this earth. You realize you have not come to this earth yet.

The Beloved creator says, my perfect child, my creation of all that is good. It is time for you to go to the human place called earth. You have chosen to go to fulfill your desire to bring some of our love, wisdom, goodness and peace to their world. I am very pleased.

What is it that you want to give that planet? What sacred contract do you want to manifest during your visit? God hands you four cards. Which of these agreements is the contract that you choose for this journey? All four will bring love, wisdom, goodness and peace. You will live all them while you are there but one speaks to you NOW. It is the one in your heart, for it is the one that will bring you love, wisdom, goodness and peace.

In this moment of contemplation—Let Spirit speak to you about the contracts you have made with yourself that do not serve you well. The ones that have NOT brought you love, wisdom, goodness and peace. In this moment discard them and create new ones. You may want to begin again with the agreement in your heart now. That is the beginning, the alpha for you. You are here to live, love, to know wisdom, goodness and peace because you are love, wisdom, goodness and peace. And so it is!

The Road Not Taken

This poem was written by Robert Frost in 1915.

Two roads diverged in a yellow wood,
And sorry I could not travel both
And be one traveler, long I stood
And looked down one as far as I could
To where it bent in the undergrowth;

Then took the other, as just as fair,
And having perhaps the better claim
Because it was grassy and wanted wear,
Though as for that the passing there
Had worn them really about the same,

And both that morning equally lay
In leaves no step had trodden black.
Oh, I marked the first for another day!
Yet knowing how way leads on to way
I doubted if I should ever come back.

I shall be telling this with a sigh
Somewhere ages and ages hence:
Two roads diverged in a wood, and I,
I took the one less traveled by,
And that has made all the difference.

Poetry like spirituality is not an absolute. It does not mean the same thing to each person. The arts and the spiritual journey are interpretive forms of the expression of our being, our own personal journey. I believe most everything in life is an interpretive experience. It can be said life is a metaphor, life is a hologram. Or as Rumi describes it,

"Each drop of the ocean, is the ocean." The word interpret, according to the thesaurus can mean unravel, unfold, reveal, clarify.

Robert Frost wrote this poem not as a reflection of his being at that moment but of a friend.

According to his unraveling and unfolding journey, he saw that there are those that no matter what choice they make, would have questions and regrets about their choice. I call it the "This Isn't It" syndrome.

At times in everyone's life there is a place where we choose a path, only to find that path did not make us happy or the outcome was not what we wanted. Mr. Frost was making the point that this is not a onetime event. There are always forks in the road of life. What we learn from our choices is what <u>makes all the difference</u>. Every day of our lives we come to "two roads diverged." Every moment we are standing at a choice point. Life is always requiring us to make choices and life also asks us to learn and grow from our choices, to unravel, reveal and unfold.

As Matthew Kelly wrote in his best-selling book, *The Rhythm of Life*, "Every moment of our lives is a crossroad. The fork in the road is constantly appearing in our lives. The ability to choose comes from our sense of purpose. Direction comes from an understanding of where we are going. Direction emerges in our lives by bringing our decisions before the altar of our essential purpose."

I like the line "Bring our decisions before the altar of essential purpose." Remember that the path we take will make "all the difference." I believe the wisest of wise is to place on the altar our essential purpose for being. At Spirit Space we have affirmed we have a purpose to reach in to reach out. We affirm that we will have a place to grow, educate and serve. We have affirmed we will meet our children's needs and that we will be a "Splendid torch to pass on to our future generations," George Bernard Shaw.

Any path that we choose will unfold, unravel and reveal things about us collectively and individually. The question is which path will demonstrate our essential purpose?

I encourage everyone to find their answers by seeking and asking questions. First ask the questions of yourself, to yourself. And when someone asks you to give them their answer, encourage them first to seek "The Kingdom Within."

We live in a society of "experts." Organized religion tells us there are experts who have the answers. Each of us must learn when we come to a "fork in the road" to make decisions that match our understanding of our purpose. This will lead to becoming the best version of the highest vision you have ever had about yourself.

I am not suggesting that we do not seek counsel from educated sources. What I do suggest is on matters of Spirit, you seek counsel from within first.

Referring back to the poem, the traveler spent much time in contemplation of one road, but took the other. Both roads seem equal in possibilities so choosing one, yet saying I will choose the other all the while, still knowing if I make that choice, I will not be able to go back.

Remembering the metaphor of the *Road Not Taken*, I ask the following questions:

- Are you making choices that reflect your essential purpose?
- Are you contemplating on the choices you are making every moment of your life?

We are always at forks in the road with the road diverging. We are always being given opportunities to go down roads less traveled. Our journey here is to know our own wholeness—whole is holiness.

Every major religion recognizes we are here on purpose for purpose. They may disagree on our purpose but where the paths converge are in giving honor to a source and contributing to highest good. The best way to do that is to identify what brings you joy and what brings joy to the world. Take that path, it is often less traveled but there will be less regrets. Know where you want to go, and then ask yourself which path will let me live my essential purpose. Once you have taken it, walk the path with joy and know that around the bend will be another diverging path.

Reasons to Go Within—Personal Application

Coaching Questions:

1. What comes up for you when you read the quote, "Bring your decisions to the altar of essential purpose"?
2. Are you making choices that reflect your essential purpose?
3. Are you contemplating the outcome that can happen as a result of the choices you are making?
4. Thinking back on your life to date, can you identify forks in the road that were crossed unconsciously?
5. Have you ever yearned for a path not chosen?

The Fire of Passion

Each of us is on this planet, at this particular time for a purpose. Our life is no coincidence. It is a series of choices that will make up our DESTINY. Purpose, Passion, Destiny and Intentions are words that are used to speak of the idea that we each come to this planet to find meaning and to discover the purpose of our existence so that we can step into our DESTINY.

Passion is what fuels our purpose. Passions are not our purpose. I firmly believe that we each have a purpose. Most of the time, we have more than one purpose as we move through our developmental stages and the evolution of our souls. Some believe that before we came to this Earth School we (our spirit) made a contract with God. The contract began with a conversation that went something like this: God says, "Well, it has been brought to my attention that you want to go to Earth School." You respond with, "Yes, I want to learn more about the human journey so my soul may evolve." God says, "Well, if that is what you want, I won't stop you. But know it will not always be easy. And once you leave the spirit world, you will not have all the super natural skills you now possess. I will send angels and guides to be with you. You know you can always call on me, but also know that while you are in Earth School you will need to learn your own lessons. Sometimes the teachers may seem harsh. Keep your heart and mind centered on your intention for leaving this peaceful, beautiful haven. Above all, you must know you are here to make earth a better place because of your presence. You will not remember this conversation." You say to God, "How will I know what it is that I am to do if I do not remember what we spoke of. What am I to DO?" God responds, "Well, every decision you make is <u>not a decision about what to do</u>, it is a decision about <u>who you are</u>! When you see this, when you come to understand this, everything will change. You will begin to see life in a new way. All events, occurrences and situations will turn into opportunities to do what you came to earth to do; to fulfill your DESTINY."

"Carefully watch your thoughts, for they become your words. Manage and watch your words, for they will become your actions. Consider and judge your actions, for they have become your habits. Acknowledge and watch your habits, for they shall become your values. Understand and embrace your values, for they become your destiny." Mahatma Gandhi

One of the co-founders and the first president of Spirit Space, Jack VandenBerg often reminds me of this quote when I speak of thoughts becoming our destiny. Remember that every spoken word has an impact on others. Every thought has an impact on you. That is why it is so important to know yourself and your intentions.

And so you decided to come here to Earth School!

Joseph Campbell said: "Life is without meaning in itself, you bring the meaning to it. The meaning of your life is whatever you ascribe it to be."

George Bernard Shaw said: "Life isn't about finding yourself, it is about creating yourself."

Ralph Waldo Emerson said: "Once you ascribe or make a decision about your life, your DESTINY, the whole universe will conspire to make it happen."

Anais Nin said: "To live is to choose. But to choose well, you must know who you are and what you stand for, where you want to go and why you want to get there."

If we are to ever awaken to our life's purpose and find the deeper meaning to our existence, we must make a committed effort to understand our true nature. When making conscious decisions that create goodness, there is one element that is always present in everyone's life purpose, that is to be a service to others and to contribute to the well-being of our planet.

In the workshops I conduct and in my coaching sessions I suggest that one must pay attention to their passions in order to discover their purpose. But remember that your passions are not your purpose! Looking at what you are passionate about provides a direction when seeking to be clear about your purpose for being.

Now, where do you want to go and why?

When we were working on creating a mission statement for Spirit Space, we knew it was going to be the core of everything we do. Our Spirit space Mission Statement is as follows: Spirit Space is an Innerfaith (ability to go within) community that inspires growth through the process of reaching in to reach out.

I will always remember Reverend Toni Boehm's Mission Statement, "I am here to be a midwife for the birthing of the soul."

Here is my mission statement: "My purpose for being is to raise spiritual consciousness, mine first and then others. I do this by teaching, serving and nurturing."

Every great achiever or humanitarian has a mission or destiny statement. Remember we are here On Purpose, For Purpose. We all have a date with Destiny.

The only way to make your date with Destiny is to live your life fully engaged.

The legend of the lady that never lived:

> There once was a woman that lived her life carefully
> She never tried to dance
> She never took a chance
> No one ever heard her laugh or cry
> She didn't dream or even try
> And on the day she passed away
> She never really lived, they say.

From *The Four Agreements*: "Our biggest fear is taking the risk to be alive, the risk to be alive and express what we really are."

The reason you live is found in every gift you give and this takes us back to the very beginning of your journey when you were in spirit speaking with God about your purpose for coming to Earth School. God said, "Above all things you must learn that your purpose is to make the earth a better place."

Gandhi put it this way: "The best way to find yourself is to lose yourself in service."

I encourage you to spend some time going within and asking yourself, Who am I? What do I stand for? Where do I want to go? Why do I want to be there? Then spend some more time going over the questions Reasons to go within—Personal application section below. There is no greater joy than to be whom you were created to be. There is no greater chaos than to be living someone else's life and not your own. And when it is all said and done, you must be yourself because everyone else is already taken.

Reasons to Go Within—Personal Application:

Coaching Questions:

What do you stand for (What are your values)?
Where do you want to go?
Why do you want to be there?
And how will it contribute and serve the world when you do?

Coaching Questions to Shine a Conscious Light on Your Passions:

1. What are you just naturally interested in?
2. What would you like to change about the world?
3. What would you like to accomplish before you die?
4. What would you do if you knew you could not fail?
5. What would you do if money was not an issue?
6. What are you currently doing that you enjoy?
7. What activities make you feel empowered?
8. What would you most like to be acknowledged for in your life?
9. If you had only one wish, what would it be?
10. Whose life and contribution do you most admire?
11. What ideas energize, inspire and excite you?
12. With whom would you like to surround yourself?
13. Do you believe you are responsible for your life and how it goes? If not you, who or what is?
14. Have you ever asked yourself, why am I here? What is my purpose? If so, what answer comes up?

The answers to these questions can help you know what is of value to you. Use this knowledge to understand your purpose. Your purpose and remember your purpose needs to be clear, concise and light filled.

Meditation:

Focus on your breath. The air being taken in and being released. Notice your body doing just what it was created to do. Give thanks.

Now, for these next few moments, I want you to imagine that the day has come for your Earth's journey to end. You are being transported back to where you began. You say goodbye to all your teachers and friends in Earth School and so it is. You arrive safely on the other side, happy to be home. There is one last thing before you start another journey. You are to listen in on the memorial service that is being held in your honor. What is it that you are hearing said about you and your journey to Earth School? What is your mission, purpose statement? When it is all said and done, you know you lived your purpose for the good of all and the evolution of your own soul. And SO IT IS!

Opportunities or Obstacles

What makes something an opportunity? What makes something an obstacle?

As Aristotle said "Excellence is never an accident. It is always the result of high intention, sincere effort, and intelligent execution; it represents the wise choice of many alternatives—choice, not chance determines your destiny." In other words it is the vision to see obstacles as opportunities.

What one sees around Spirit Space is a perfect example of what could have been perceived as too many obstacles but instead we chose to see them as an opportunity. Many of our most difficult moments, the things that seem almost impossible or overwhelming are really opportunities. Renovating a hair salon into a sanctuary on a limited budget in one month presented quite a few challenges. (Oh, I mean opportunities.)

There were many opportunities to learn, to grow, to share, to connect, to develop compassion and empathy, to develop new skill sets, to see what stuff we are really made of. Joseph Campbell said "Opportunities to find deeper powers within ourselves come when life seems most challenging." Those challenging moments are called "Trouble at the border" in coaching.

Just know that whenever you are close to coming into your promise land, the place of achieving your heart's desires, allowing your spirit to soar, there will be TROUBLE AT THE BORDER.

The good news is that you are really close to achieving your goal because you cannot have trouble at the border unless you are at the border. Often times the closer you are to achieving your goal, you will experience this "Oh no—I will never make it" attitude. It is the monkey talk or in others words, these are the times we think "I cannot accomplish this goal." Don't let those monkeys dressed up as border guards stop you!

Is it Opportunity or Obstacle? If you cross over then it was an opportunity. If you turn back or give up then it becomes an obstacle.

There will never be a way to measure how many great visions were never realized, never developed into reality because the opportunity was seen as an obstacle.

In Chinese, the word crisis is composed of two characters. One represents danger, the other opportunity.

I often refer to the primitive part of our brain that is all about danger and survival as the monkey mind. It includes a radar system that is always scoping out danger, although most of the time it is perceived danger not real danger. If you allow this most primitive mind, a mind disconnected from your Spirit to run the show, opportunities will turn into fear which will be perceived as danger or obstacles.

"We have not been given a spirit of fear." 2 Timothy 1-7. Fear is not a spiritual birthright.

Jonathan Lockwood Huie said:

> "Our opportunity is to Soar our Spirit.
> To see light and joy in everything.
> To spread our wings and fly boldly
> To give thanks for rainbows and butterflies our symbols of
> renewal and rebirth."

Opportunity is to soar our Spirit!

I believe our choices create opportunities. Every moment of our lives we are called to make choices that create opportunities. We get to choose how we will respond to any given situation. We get to choose whether we see rain or rainbows. We get to live a life that is filled with possibilities and gratitude or live one that is filled with despair and cynicism.

It is our choice as to how we will perceive any given situation. Winston Churchill described a pessimist and an optimist this way: "A pessimist sees the difficulty in every opportunity. An optimist sees the opportunity in every difficulty." Opportunity or Obstacle?

Ralph Waldo Emerson reminds us to "Never lose an opportunity of seeing anything beautiful for beauty is the handwriting of God." God's handwritten messages are everywhere all of the time. Our willingness to see them is our choice.

We need to decide what we will do with those moments in life (and we all have them) when we get to choose to let our Spirit Soar. We must then choose to not allow fear and perceived limitations to stop us from crossing over into the Promise Land.

I like the phrase Promise Land. It comes from an Old Testament Bible story about Moses and the Israelites. For 40 years the Israelites wandered in the desert looking for the promise land, the land that they believed their God had promised them. The more they grumbled and complained, the more they left the truth of who their God was and what their God promised, the longer they spent in the desert, forty years! There were a series of mountain top experiences and many valley experiences. Israel is not exactly a large country so some have speculated they were probably walking in circles. Metaphorically they were unconscious of what was all around them. They repeated the same story, walked in the same footsteps, learned very little and grumbled a lot. We need to become aware of the walking in circles game. When we come to understand we are not getting anywhere, we can stop and remember who we really are, what we really want and who God really is.

As soon as we recognize this, we often have an aha moment. When that happens we can stop the circling and get to our destination. Is it an Opportunity or an Obstacle?

Reasons to Go Within—Personal Application

Coaching Questions:

1. Is there some place in your life that you see as a perceived block, or obstacle? Is it keeping you from your highest? Just for now, consider that this is an opportunity. How are you going to use this as an opportunity?
2. Is there some Trouble at the Border in your life?
3. Are you wandering around in the barren emptiness of the desert when in front of you is the Promise Land?
4. Are there monkeys dressed up as border guards chattering in your head, saying that you can never have all that is your Divine birthright? What do they say? Do you believe that your dreams and aspirations can come true if you stay connected to the opportunity and disconnect from the obstacle mindset? How can you achieve that?

Affirm right now that you are an AMAZING creation of God and the desires of your heart are the contracts you and God have promised to co-create for highest good. Look for opportunities to make choices that will lead you to your promise land!

Meditation

In the quiet place of your heart, just breath, release any perceived danger. Know that God did not give you a Spirit of Fear or discouragement but a Spirit that longs to Soar.

> See rainbows not storms
> See sunshine not clouds
> See moonbeams not dark nights
> See love not fear
> See hope not despair
> See forgiveness not resentment
> See thankfulness not lack
> See opportunities not obstacles
> Rainbows
> Sunshine
> Moonbeams
> Hope
> Forgiveness
> Thankfulness
> Opportunities

Breathe in the divine energy that these words represent

> Rainbows—God's promise—Opportunity
> Sunshine—God's light
> Moonbeams—God's light
> Love—God's promise
> Hope—God's promise
> Forgiveness—God's promise
> Thankfulness—God's gift

Welcome your soul to the Promise Land.

Come As You Are Party

I bought a new steam cleaner for my floors recently and as I opened the box I read the promo on it, it read this way: "You deserve to have the best cleaning experience possible . . ."

We live in a society that is always telling us what we deserve, don't we? Think about it . . . You deserve the best partner, the best lifestyle, the best car, the best health, the best job, the best hamburger, etc. Please do not take this wrong, but WHAT? Does this mean someone else does not deserve it? What makes any of us think we deserve ANYTHING or NOTHING? This is an interesting thought is it not?

And if we do not have the best this or that, does that mean we do not deserve it?

Well, New Thought principles teach us that we all are deserving of all good things. Why? It is because we have a contract with our Creator. Another way of looking at this is to say we have an invitation to experience the best party of all times. And the reason you are invited is because <u>of</u> your relationship to the Cosmic Party Host. It is not because you did anything, it is because you are someone special, and EVERYONE else is too!

So play with me a bit. You go to your computer, you are going through the loads of emails that came in during the night and you see an EVITE. Now, I am an old fashion girl, so I go to the post office and as I am walking out of the Post Office, I thumb through the piles of paper and I see a special envelope with some sort of invitation.

OK, now we all are looking at our invitations. It says that you are cordially invited to a Cosmic Universe Party. Oh My Goodness! Me, I am invited . . .

First, you may think—What did I do to deserve (keep an eye on this word deserve,) such an invitation? For you know it is going to be the most grand, amazing party of the year, heck in eternity. Who would not want to be invited to this party?

"Oh, what should I wear?" I must show up looking spectacular. Maybe you think, "I do not know what is appropriate for such an occasion." You may start off thinking that this is all a mistake. "How did I get invited to this party? Should I just go and sort of fake it or pretend my way through it even though I may feel like an imposter through the whole event." (As if no one will notice the mistake.) You start hoping that no one finds out that you do not deserve to be here, then your mind starts playing out scenarios. "I have to practice what I am going to say." OH MY!

Then you read the details of the invitation and you see in Big Bold LETTERS, **COME AS YOU ARE, NOW!**

Oh, there is a problem. I cannot possibly come as I am **NOW**, especially **NOW.** I am not prepared, not polished enough. I have to clean myself up. At this point, one could walk away feeling very confused, angry and sad.

You might think, "I am so confused, why did I even get this invitation if I cannot go?" You may think, "I am so mad, why would the Cosmic Host throw such a party? What a stupid idea." **COME AS YOU ARE, NOW!**

You may start feeling sad knowing you are going to miss the biggest, grandest time of your life because you are not prepared. OK, I suspect most of you now understand my analogy. God invites us each and eve₁y moment of our life to the grandest party. All God asks is that <u>we come as we are NOW</u>, not some day, NOW. There is no need to look a certain way, speak a certain way, and behave a certain way. All that is required is that you accept the invitation and <u>Come as You Are</u>.

The invitation is yours even when you feel you are not good enough, smart enough or deserving enough. The invitation is there when you feel on top of the world, even those times when you think you do not need God and that you have it all under control. The invitation still reads <u>Come as You Are</u>. The invitation comes when you are feeling at your lowest. There is no mistake about this invitation. There is no time restriction, there is no dress code, there is just this beautiful ongoing, forever open invitation by God to <u>Come as You Are</u>, because who you are is not about anything of this world. It is about your essence, your energy. Your spirit which is always prepared, always beautifully robed, always intelligent, wise and knowing.

I would say there is a no such thing as deserving in our Creator's language. Why? Because to have a deserving says there is an undeserving and that is NOT THE TRUTH! There is no undeserving. Of course there is a "Reap what you sow" principle, cause and effect, but no undeserving.

In a perfect world we all would get this; there would be no advertising saying, "You deserve the best" or "You deserve a break today." Our Creator only sees good or better not deserving or undeserving.

What would it be like for all of us, as co-creators, if we only chose to see good or better in place of deserving or undeserving? What if we chose to see this in each other, in situations, in difficult times or experiences? Without exceptions our world would shift.

Do you see that we could not only be different ourselves, but we would make a difference? Let me tell you the story of the two little girls who asked their daddy for a pony for Christmas. When they awoke on Christmas morning, they ran outside only to find two piles of manure. The one little girl started crying. She said, "I asked for a pony and all I got was a pile of pony pooh." The other little girl said, "Let's start digging, with all this pony poop, there has to be a pony here somewhere."

Whenever the pony pooh shows up in piles for me, I remind myself of that story. I want to be the one who looks for the pony or looks for the good, don't you?

Life does leave us some piles, it is a sure thing, but what if there is a pony wherever there are piles of pony pooh?

So, are you ready to show up for the Come as You Are Party? The Cosmic Host, Spirit, The Divine Energy is waiting for your response. Do not let words and thoughts such as, "I am not deserving, I am not yet ready" stop you from experiencing the wonder and excitement that is awaiting.

We all have a sacred contract and the only way to fulfill it is to show up. Show up expecting Great and Mighty Things. Come to the party of life that you and God have created.

One way to do that is to start your day saying, "I accept your invitation God, I am ready to party just as I am." When I say party, it means you have accepted the invitation to be fully present and you will not question your worthiness or readiness. There is no preparation required except to be willing to let Spirit lead you. You are all about celebration. As Oprah said, "The more you praise and celebrate your life, the more there is in life to celebrate." So parties are always about celebration and celebration is an expression of gratitude. Celebrate, knowing that you are fully, truly whole, Holy.

Reasons to Go Within—Personal Application

Coaching Questions:

1. How would you respond if you knew you were invited to God's party?
2. What do you believe about deserving and undeserving?
3. If everyone agrees there is no undeserving, then is there truly a deserving? If we eliminate deserving from our vocabulary, what is another word that could be used in its place?
4. How would you see the world shifting if we gave up the idea of deserving and underserving?
5. How do you incorporate karma into this thought?
6. Can you imagine getting the invitation to Come As You Are for the ultimate Come As You Are party, passing from this life to the next? What would be your first thought? What does your response say to you? Have you planned what you need to be ready for this party?

Meditation:

Breathe—Relax—Let the energy of the Spirit move through you. In your mind's eye—see the invitation written and sent to you with the greatest love. Spend a moment, a few breaths being so thankful to receive the invitation to participate in co-creating each day as if it were a grand cosmic party to celebrate. The party of wonder, gratitude, and excitement for each new day, each opportunity to love, to live, to laugh. To serve, to contribute, to make known for all others that they are invited too. And So It Is.

Celebrate Life

When God gives me a topic to co-create for a Reasoning, I know that I will have opportunities to experience those teachings in my own life. This is often a sobering thought.

What I mean, is when a thought or direction comes from God such as speaking on forgiveness, I then know situations will come up where I can choose to practice forgiveness or not. But the choice will be placed in front of me; the purpose will be made clear. For everything that comes up for each of us in this lifetime is an opportunity to practice, learn, grow and, become more conscious. We can choose whether we will learn the lesson now or later, but we will learn.

When Spirit spoke to me about doing a Reasoning on Celebrating Life, I was tickled. OK, God—this means I am going to have opportunities to celebrate life myself. I was ready to put my party pants on.

The opportunity to choose to celebrate life did not come as I expected. The balloons got popped; the confetti was made not of colorful paper particles but bitter herbs. What I was presented with was the opportunity to sit at the bedside of a dying spiritual sister who a month earlier was creating a vision for her life.

I also had the opportunity to hold an exhausted spiritual sister who was told of the choices to attempt to prolong her young life. I sat with another spiritual sister as she buried her beloved mother and asked the question, "How do I live in a world without a mother? I have always had a mother."

I spent time coaching and ministering to another young mother as she began chemotherapy. And I thought, is this a cosmic joke? I am preparing to speak on the Celebration of Life while being emerged in the Bitter Herbs of Life.

No, it is no cosmic joke!

The celebration of life happens in all forms and in all ways. As I sat by Mary's bedside, they said she was unconscious, but she heard me as I celebrated her life. I remembered who she was, I heard her laughter in my very being and I saw her tears and fears through the years. I remembered her visions and dreams, her accomplishments, her joys. I celebrated life that moment with Mary.

What does it mean to celebrate life? These experiences allowed me to see another side of the wisdom of celebrating life. It reminded me of the importance of living each moment, being fully present, fully engaged, fully aware that this moment is the only one the counts because it is the only one we are sure of.

"I am reaching out to feel the infinite. I am reaching out to know the divine. Forever is already mine. I am already there, I'm already home." This is a great New Thought song, "I'm Reaching Out" by Daniel Nahmod. I like the words because there are so many songs and writings that speak as if happiness is always something in the future. NO! Happiness comes from Celebrating the Here, the NOW—Embracing JOY, the joys of this present moment. Happiness does not come from circumstances, it comes from the heart.

I celebrate your presence here—each of you

I celebrate Spirit Space and all the possibilities that it presents us

I celebrate the air I am breathing

My heart beating

I celebrate this wonderful, diverse community we share.

I join Walt Whitman when he declared, "I celebrate myself!" In this moment, what are you celebrating?

Charles Fillmore said that life for each of us should be a "Journey in jubilance."

Thomas Carlyle said "Every day that is born into this world comes like a burst of music and rings the whole day through and you make of it a dance, a dirge or a life march, as you choose."

The word celebrate means to honor, recognize and rejoice in.

Eric Butterworth said, "In celebrating consciousness, you look around and bless your family, friends, coworkers, fellow travelers along the journey of life. Bless the sunshine, the clouds, the trees, grass and flowers. Without this sense of celebration, you are poor no matter what your net worth may be."

Erma Bombeck wrote these words in the 2 December 1979 column titled "If I Had to Live My Life Over":

Instead of wishing away nine months of pregnancy and complaining about the shadow over my feet, I'd have cherished every minute of it and realized that the wonderment growing inside me was to be my only chance in life to assist God in a miracle.

I would have cried and laughed less while watching television . . . and more while watching life.

I would have gone to bed when I was sick, instead of pretending the Earth would go into a holding pattern if I weren't there for a day.

There would have been more I love yous . . . more I'm sorrys . . . more I'm listenings . . . but mostly, given another shot at life, I would seize every minute of it . . . look at it and really see it . . . try it on . . . live it . . . exhaust it . . . and never give that minute back until there was nothing left of it.

You can read the full original article as well as an internet circulated version on the following website: http://www.snopes.com/glurge/bombeck.asp.

In Edmund Rostand's classic work, *The Chanticleer*, he tells the poignant story of a rooster who crowed lustily every morning at sunrise, he actually thought it was <u>his</u> crowing that caused the sun to rise. It gave him a sense of significance. His life mattered, his passion being served.

One morning he overslept. He rushed to his post atop the hen house only to find the sun had already risen without him. His dream world collapsed as he realized the truth. It was a delusion—"I serve no purpose," he thought. But then, to his mind came the wisdom of the ages, "All my crowing does not cause the sun to rise, but my crowing is to celebrate the sun rising."

We are here to celebrate the sun rising and setting. To celebrate the changing of seasons. To celebrate, love, joy, peace, passion, compassion and hope. What would you be doing differently if you began each sunrise crowing celebration, the celebration of your life? What would your life look like if you celebrated your life, your purpose, your intention?

In the meditation from the Reasoning titled "The Fire of Passion" I ask you to get a vision of your intention for the year. Two of Mother Teresa's intention statements are: "From the moment a soul has the grace to know God, she must seek." "Give of your hands to serve and your hearts to love."

Here is my intention statement:

> I am English and Russian Jew by blood
> This is who I am by birth
> I am an American by citizenship
> This is where my citizenship lies
> I am a pastor, therapist, coach, wife, mother and friend
> My calling is to be a Spiritual Teacher/healer, to be a contribution
> This is my vocation
> My heart's desire is to know God intimately
> This is my purpose

What is your intention statement?

If you would like to share it, please post it at avoiceofreasonbook.com.

I ask that you take a moment and go into silence with a notebook in hand. Ask Spirit to give you a vision of how you want to celebrate your life. What would your life look like if a celebrant? Embrace JOY. Cultivate LOVE. What would your invitation to the Celebration of Life look like? Write your I am statements.

Reason to Go Within—Personal Application

Coaching Questions:

1. Walt Whitman said, "I celebrate myself." What does this statement mean to you? How do you celebrate yourself?
2. Erma Bombeck wrote "If I had to do my life over." Write yours.
3. Create your intention statement beginning with I am.

Oprah's Reasoning—Words of Success

The inspiration for this Reasoning came from Oprah and our Spirit Space administrator, Sal. We were sitting at meditation on Wednesday, May 25th, 2011. I had just arrived in Saugatuck after my week in Chicago. People were sharing and Sal said something to the effect of "I watched Oprah's farewell show and what I experienced was something that felt just like Spirit Space. It was as if I was sitting in Spirit Space and I was listening to a Reasoning." When I got home I watched the late night version of the Oprah show and I understood what Sal was saying. Oprah's words, her delivery, the intention—that is just what happens each Sunday at Spirit Space. For those who saw this show, think of the energy that was created. And for those who missed it, let me share parts of what I considered one of the most inspiring truth filled Reasonings I have ever heard.

I believe God and Oprah contracted or co-created her Earth School experience in such a way that we all could understand that anyone from anywhere can make a difference. "There are no coincidences, only Divine Order," is one of Oprah Winfrey's hallmark messages.

Oprah said: "I am truly amazed that I, who started out in rural Mississippi in 1954 when the vision for a black girl was limited to being a maid or a teacher in a segregated school, could end up here." Oprah went on to say, "Because this is my calling, what I know for sure from this experience is that we are ALL CALLED."

We all have a calling, a contract, a purpose, a destiny. Oprah's life gives us an opportunity to remember that there can be no excuses as to why you are not living your passion. That is why this message to the world came in the form of a very human, very real person. She isn't a beauty queen or super model or heiress. She is an African

American woman, born in the south during a challenging time in our history—she did not have the protection of her parents to keep her safe from sexually abusive men and physically abusive forms of discipline. What she had was a knowing deep within her being that she was here to make a difference in the world. AND SO ARE YOU!

Oprah said "Each of you has a platform. Do not let my trappings here fool you. Mine is a stage in a studio. Yours is wherever you are within your own reach, however small or however large that reach is. Maybe it is 20 people, maybe its 30 people or 40 people. Wherever you are, that is your platform, your stage, your circle of influence. That is your talk show and that is where your power lies."

When I heard the numbers she was stating, I could not help but think that she was speaking to Spirit Space. We were in that number range at the time of this Reasoning. We began just that way.

Oprah went on to say, "You can help somebody, you can listen, you can forgive, you can heal. You have the power to change someone's life. You are letting your life speak for you and when you do that, you will receive in direct proportion to how you give."

We have a platform here at Spirit Space to use our gifts to give in the proportion that we receive. And we each have a personal platform as well. And we all have been given SO MUCH!

Oprah spoke a little of the early beginnings in Chicago and that too reminds me of Spirit Space. She said to the person who hired her, "Will there be an audience?" In the beginning days of Spirit Space I asked my boss (God), "Will there be an audience?" Oprah went on to say, "After our first show, we put up some folding chairs." That is what Spirit Space did. Oprah went on to say "We gathered a staff, as pitiful as it was, we would bribe people with coffee and doughnuts.

Then the word spread. Have you seen that black girl on TV named Oprah?"

This is what some have been saying about Spirit Space. "Have you heard about that new Spiritual Enrichment Center on Blue Star Highway?"

What is the lesson on Passion and Purpose that Oprah shared? It is that we all have a calling, a purpose and we will receive in direct proportion to what we give. We have our own platform, we have our own talents. We are manifestors.

What is the lesson on <u>Responsibility?</u> Oprah said, "You are responsible for your own life. What is life? It is ENERGY. It is energy and we are transmitting it all the time and the world is responding in kind. You are responsible for the energy you create. Do not wait for someone else to fix you, change you or complete you. It is yours to do, only then are you free." Oprah then quoted Dr. Jill Bolt Taylor, the brain scientist who suffered a stroke and became aware of the energy of others during her recovery process. Dr. Jill Taylor said, "Take responsibility for the energy you bring into this space." Her book is titled *My Stroke of Insight*.

If you come into a space and you do not like the energy, check out the energy you bring to that space. Or if a space has good energy and you feel it shift, take responsibility to shift it back by checking your energy. Often we have every intention of being and bringing good energy into a conversation and then we put out a negative or limiting statement without even knowing it until we feel the shift. Dr. Taylor says "Check and make sure you are aware of your responsibility for any shift." And Oprah adds, "Nobody but you is responsible for your life. It doesn't matter what your mama did! It doesn't matter what your Daddy didn't do!"

Because you are here right now, it means you are worthy. We must stop the self-destructive cycle of blocking our own blessings because we do not feel inherently good enough, smart enough, pretty enough, worthy enough. *It is our birthright to be worthy.* Yet, there is a common thread that runs through our pain and suffering, it is a sense of unworthiness.

On that topic, Marianne Williamson said: "Our deepest fear is not that we are inadequate. Our deepest fear is that we are powerful beyond measure. It is our light, not our darkness, that most frightens us. We ask ourselves, who am I to be, brilliant, gorgeous, talented and/or fabulous? Actually, who are you not to be? You are a child of God. Your playing small does not serve the world. There is nothing enlightened about shrinking so that other people won't feel insecure around you. We are all meant to shine, as children do. We were born to manifest the glory of God that is within us. It's not just in some of us; it's in everyone. And as we let our own light shine, we unconsciously give other people permission to do the same. As we are liberated from our own fear, our presence automatically liberates others."

Because of this thread of unworthiness that seems to weave us all together, we have difficulty showing up BIG—so we shrink so others will not be threatened or threaten us. We need to stop playing small! I believe part of being an advanced student of Earth School is to know your worthiness. Even when validation is not present, it must not cause you to question your worth, value and energy that you bring to the world.

There is not one of us who does not question our worth from time to time when we are in need of validation. Please remember, you are always worthy.

Everyone shines brighter when validated. We all want it and do better when we receive it. The hook comes when we NEED it to know we are OK. That puts us at the mercy of another's energy. Remember, anything that is given or seen is a reflection of the giver more than the receiver. May we as students of Earth School say as Carrie from Ann Arbor said about The Oprah show, "Watching you be yourself makes me want to be more of myself."

What is your secret to success? Oprah's answer, "My team and Jesus, because nothing but the hand of God has made this possible for me. And for all of you who get riled up when I mention God (Jesus) and you want to know which God I am talking about, I am talking about the same one you talk about. I am talking about the Alpha and Omega, the omniscient, the omnipresent, the ultimate consciousness, the source, the force, the all of everything there is, the one and only GOD." WOW! That is the God Spirit Space talks about because there is only one God. And it comes in many disguises.

Oprah also spoke of the Grace of the One. It is as close as your breath, it is always present. Be still and know it. You can acknowledge it or not, you can worship it or not, you can praise it, you can ignore it or you can know it.

In summary, Oprah's Reasoning on May 25th, 2011 came to Spirit Space on July 24th, 2011. Through this Reasoning:

- Lesson #1
  o We are all called—We are all here on purpose for purpose
  o Wherever we are, that is our studio/stage/platform
- Lesson #2
  o Life is energy
  o We are responsible for the energy we bring into any space

- Lesson #3
    o Give in direct proportion to what has been given to you
    o Acknowledge the grace and guidance of God always present

And SO IT IS!!

Reason to go within—Personal application

Coaching Questions:

1. We are all called for a purpose—Do you know your calling?
2. What does it mean to you to be responsible for the energy you bring into a space?
3. How can you personally shift energy?
4. We receive in direct proportion to what we give. Where in your life has that been demonstrated? Is there some place in your life where you can create this reciprocal effect more consistently?
5. How do you honor the grace that is always present in your life?

Section II

Jewels in your Heart's Crown

Jewels in your Heart's Crown Introduction

This set of Reasonings comes from the metaphor of your heart wearing a crown. On this crown are four jewels. The crown is part of our soul's yearning for intimacy, deep connections and relationships. Relationships can be the most rewarding aspect of living yet it is also the most difficult to master. Our greatest moments involve matters of the heart, as does our deepest sorrows. How do we experience the power of the crown that sets on our heart?

Matters of the Heart—Trust

The tradition of Valentine's Day is about love and relationships. Let's take a closer look at relationships and love. Love and connection is not just about a season or a day. Love is present always. A great example of this is the creation of Spirit Space. Spirit Space was created because of relationships. It was not created because of a doctrine or even a dilemma as some may think. It came about because of a need to stay connected to each other which is the energy of love. A need to stay connected is love.

Many of you may remember the classic movie Love Story with Ally McGraw and Ryan O'Neil. There was this line in the movie, "Love means you never have to say you are sorry." We all know that is absolutely <u>not</u> true. Love means you get the opportunity to say you are sorry over and over and over again. The line does have some interesting aspects, for you see, many people think that relationships should be EASY and that is what that statement infers to me. Most of us <u>know</u> relationships are not easy. They challenge us in ways that nothing else can. Do they not?

Relationships can hurt us deeply. They can cause us to behave in ways that make us hardly recognize ourselves or others. You may find yourself asking, "Did I just do that? Did I just say that? What was I thinking?"

Relationships can offer us our deepest blows and our most amazing, joyful experiences. When it is all said and done, <u>everything</u> is about relationships. There are the relationships we have with others, the relationship we have with our self and the relationship we have with God. As I said everything is about relationships.

This is a good time to remind you of my workshop entitled Creating Conscious Relationships. It is well worth setting aside a day in your life dedicated to the understanding of yourself in relationships whether via my workshop or elsewhere. This workshop provides an opportunity to learn skills that can enhance your relationships by knowing yourself better. You can find a current list of workshop offerings on avoiceofreasonbook.com.

Relationships are something that are all inclusive and very important yet seem to be baffling, ambiguous and filled with myths and misconceptions. We often seem to lack understanding, education and skills to maintain healthy relationships. We are taught to do math problems, science theories, how to conjugate verbs, yet there are no classes in school that teach us about the most important things in life, relationships and love. The metaphor of a heart represents love and our hearts wear a crown. The crown has many jewels and we will look at four of them. Each jewel is an aspect of Love. These jewels are Trust—Respect—Acceptance—Responsibility. I have created Reasonings to address each of these topics. They are the four crown jewels.

TRUST

I think everyone would agree that the foundation for a loving, healthy relationship is trust. But, what is trust? Where does it come from? Is there a difference between TRUST and TRUSTING in someone or something? What do you need to be able to trust? Do you need to trust someone to feel safe with them? Or can you not fully trust someone and yet still feel safe and still love them unconditionally? Let's begin by addressing the question, what is trust?

The American Heritage Dictionary defines trust as "a <u>firm</u> and <u>hopeful</u> reliance on the fidelity, integrity or ability of a person or thing." The problem with this definition is there are two words that are used that seem somewhat opposite—firm and hopeful. If I am firm, I am not hoping, I know. The experts of definition are not so sure about this word TRUST either.

We usually use TRUST as a noun, as if it is a mental reality. Remember nouns describe persons, places and things. Actually, trust makes more sense when we use it as a verb. Trust is a process. It is not a feeling. It begins where all things begin, in a belief. What you believe about Trust, Relationships and yourself will create your definition of Trust.

There are those who believe that trust is earned. There are those who believe that trust is there until proven unwarranted. There are those who believe you can never fully trust anyone ever. There are those who believe trust is always about the other person.

David Richo shares much wisdom in his bestseller *How to Be an Adult in Relationships*. In his book *Daring to Trust*, he speaks of relationships coming in two forms, the childlike relationships and the adult version. He gives a checklist of the Adult belief system of TRUST.

- I trust myself to receive the trustworthiness of others.
- I trust myself to handle betrayal by others without vindictiveness.
- I trust my own intuition and what the record shows about each person, a situation, not on promises or wishful thinking.
- I commit myself to being unconditionally trustworthy toward others, no matter how anyone ever acts toward me.
- I see that to be trustworthy does not mean that I have to be rigidly reliable but only reliably real.

All of us have been hurt, lied to and about, deceived or let down. When that happens our humanness wants to recoil, become fearful, not take risks and become untrusting. So what is the answer? If TRUST is the foundation for all relationships and we all have been hurt and want to avoid being hurt again, how can we TRUST? How can we have loving relationships?

Iyanla Vanzant in *Until Today* said "Trust is a simple process. Either you trust or you don't trust. You either trust yourself or you don't trust yourself. When you don't trust yourself, you will not trust other people. When you do not trust other people, you cannot trust the process of living or loving in which other people are involved. When you are not open to living fully, it means that you expect to be hurt. This expectation makes you constantly afraid that you can't handle the pain. When you don't believe you can handle something, it means you don't trust yourself." This is exactly where we started, isn't it?

First, we must build our own inner resources so that our safety and security lie stably within ourselves, not based on others. We need to trust our self even more than being concerned about trusting others. Second, we must develop an unconditional yes to life as it is! Third, we must continue on a path of developing a deeper relationship with God, the Infinite or whatever you choose to call it.

Let's look at each of these "We must statements" for a moment: A path of trust happens when we build a relationship with our self. It is when we love and trust our self. This is when we trust our own capabilities to handle whatever life brings. Pema Chödrön in *Taking the Leap: Freeing Ourselves From Old Habits and Fears* puts it this way, "The path of loving—kindness has the meaning of trusting oneself—trusting that we have what it takes to know ourselves thoroughly and completely without feeling hopeless, without turning against ourselves for what we see." So we must have the ability to see our flaws and not turn against ourselves. We must trust our own journey. Han Hung, the 8th century poet said "The biggest risk is to trust that these conditions are all that I need to become myself and my highest self." I think that TRUST is more about our self than others, don't you? If we trust our self we will not be so concerned about trusting others. The only way to trust yourself is to know yourself, your highest self, your divine holy spirit that is ever present within. When I see people in my practice that have been hurt and are trying to learn to trust again, the first thing that I do is have them look within. When I am hurt by the humanness of life and my own relationships, I ask myself to look within for the strength and answers.

The next step is to develop an unconditional Yes to Life as it is. This means living life in the present, not from the past, being fully present to all the possibilities that are ours in this moment. Saying Yes to Life as it is means living in this moment and Letting Go and Letting Life Happen. It allows the energy of this present moment to have more power than any past moment. Saying Yes to Life as it is in this moment reminds us that within each of us is the gift of the universe. The gift is an ability to make something good and useful out of the worst of situations, it is called the power of human spirit. Saying Yes means we refuse to see ourselves as victims but as pilgrims on an adventure that is filled with excitement and of course some unexpected events as any adventure produces. As with any pilgrimage, everything does not always go as planned, yet we accept it all as part of a grand plan.

Lastly, trust is a result of developing a deep connection to the Infinite, our creator, God.

Faith is what trust looks like when it transcends. It is all that has happened, all that is seen, or thought. Hebrew 11:1 "Faith is the substance of things hoped for, the evidence of things not seen." In *Return to Love*, by Marianne Williamson, she says "To trust in the force that moves the universe is faith. Faith isn't blind, it's visionary. Faith is believing that the universe is on our side, and that the universe knows what it is doing."

When we join our hearts in a faith based reality with our own trust in ourselves and say yes to life as it is, we are on a transcendent plane with Thy Will Be Done or I Am One With Thy Will. It then can be said that every experience is an epiphany. It is a realization that God and I are one. We are not separate. As Thomas Keating put it: "Though we are not God, God and our true self are the same thing."

This beautiful jewel that is placed in the crown, TRUST—is in all of our crowns. For you see it is not based on what has happened to you or what was done to you. It is based on your true nature which is God's true nature. We are all capable of trust. It is more of a question of what are we trusting in, others or our self and God? If you trust yourself and God, you will see others differently.

Reasons to Go Within—Personal Application

Coaching Questions:

1. Do you believe trust comes from faith? What must you have faith in to trust?
2. Explain the difference between being reliably real versus rigidly reliable. How does this difference show up in your life?
3. How does one build self-trust?

Matters of the Heart—Respect

We just visited the jewel of TRUST that sits on our Heart Throne. I am referring to the heart as the metaphor for the source of love within. I describe this place called heart as one of the places Spirit dwells. When we feel something deeply we often say I feel it in my heart. I most often sign my letters and notes, From My Heart or Love From My Heart to Yours. This is where I try to operate much of the time. Now let's visit the jewel in our heart's crown—Respect.

When the Board of Spirit Space first gathered I asked each member what they thought their gift was that they were bringing as a board member. I remember thinking, what is it that I can offer? My answer was, "I will come from My Heart. Whatever I do, it will be generated from my heart." I thought what better thing can I offer than my love. And I do not know how to do it any other way. Spirit Space was created out of love. Love for each other. I said this earlier but it bears repeating, "We were created out of the desire to be together not out of a doctrine or a dilemma or discord, but out of the relationships that had been formed from the heart." Our hearts missed each other so we gathered. Remember there is a Spirit Space within. This space is your sacred gathering place.

Our hearts on some deep intuitive knowing sensed we could not, NOT be together. Our hearts just would not allow it. Isn't that how some of you felt when you met your partner or a love of your life? It is as if you just could not see yourself without them. That is how love and matters of the heart work. That is also how our spiritual enrichment center, Spirit Space works. This is some of the magic of Spirit Space; we are about people and not doctrine. And we all know that this mystical metaphor, the heart can not only love deeply but it can feel as if it is breaking. This can happen when an event comes into our life that causes us great loss, or when someone or something hurts us deeply.

Our Emotional Hearts are as amazing as our physical hearts are, they are strong enough to do great acts of kindness and courage and generosity. And yet melt in the presence of a child or feel like breaking at a perceived betrayal. Our heart can feel as if it is about to break in two and yet be willing to mend and go on to Love again, to Trust again.

Yet, in order for a heart to function at its highest and its <u>Best</u>, it must be treated with the jewel of <u>Respect</u>. The second jewel on our crown is Respect. I am sure we could all gather many great examples of what Respect is. We all certainly know when we are being respected and when we are not, don't we? Respect can be as simple as a look or as complicated as boundaries. Certainly, Respect is being considerate of another's rights, views, desires, even if they are not ours. Yet, we know that Respect is so much more than just allowing others freedom to be. We can follow all those guidelines and still not respect the person. Maybe we just complied with or acknowledged their views, desires or rights. But the Respect that comes from the heart center is much more than that. When we speak of love, we are speaking of Love for OURSELF, OTHERS AND GOD.

When I wrote about TRUST in the previous Reasoning, I wrote of the need to TRUST our self and God as being far more powerful than the need to trust others. If you trust yourself and God, you will know when it is safe to be with someone. The jewel of Respect has that same characteristic. If you Respect Yourself and Your God, Respecting Others will be a <u>given</u>. Buddha said: "You as much as anyone in the universe deserve <u>your</u> love and respect." Jesus said: "Love yourself as your neighbor." Remember, we are all one.

For you see when you respect yourself you would not want to violate your principles or your values. When you are living in your own integrities, you will automatically be respectful of others. Buddha put it this way: "Like a caring mother, holding and guarding the life of her only child, so with a boundless heart, hold yourself and all beings."

It has been said, if you do not respect yourself, you cannot fully respect others. The same is said of trust and the same is said of love.

To understand this more fully, consider the times you have been in one of those "not so pretty places" of being critical and down on yourself. During those times, how friendly and loving are you feeling toward others? NOT VERY! How much do you have to give? NOT MUCH! For this is the principle of oneness, our interconnectedness is made so clear. We are all connected like links in a beautiful gold necklace; each link is as important as the next and if one link gets weak and breaks, the whole necklace is affected and compromised.

We are here by an infinite plan, divinely connected. We are here to uplift and support ourselves, others, the community which we live and the world. Our divine calling and purpose is to love and respect one another so that prosperity reaches the lives of all. It is the prosperity of goodness, support and creativity.

Love and Respect are linked just as much as Trust and Faith are linked. Which comes first? In a Jewish marriage the groom pledges to be a good and faithful husband by saying these words "I will work for you, respect you sustain you." Notice the word Love is left out. We often will say, "Well isn't it love that unites them?" In Jewish culture it is often thought that it is Respect that unites them and out of Respect comes Love, not the other way around. I tend to agree.

When we speak of the importance of self-love, maybe it could be even more effective to speak of it as self-respect. For if you respect yourself, you will be more aware of what does not feel respectful to you and consequently you will be more respectful of others. Respect thrives when we value and maintain the individuality of the human spirit as uniquely and divinely created. It has often been said that love is more egocentric because when we love we often expect to be loved back, but respect is <u>really</u> Loving back.

How respecting and loving are you to yourself? Do you say unkind, disrespectful things to yourself? Do you value and respect your individual views, needs and desires? Do you respect the Creator of you? If you are harsh and judgmental of yourself, where does God fit into the spectrum? For you see, you did not create yourself. You make choices as to how you are going to live your life but you <u>are</u> a magnificent creation of God. God created you. You came here by divine inspiration.

Sure, we do not always act like perfect creations of God but often <u>Being</u> and <u>Behaving</u> can be two distinctly different things. Our essence, the Being is our ontological, highest self. Our God created perfection. The Behaving is the actions and choices we make which are often done without consulting our higher self. That is when we can get ourselves into some disrespectful places, it is when we do not consult our inner wisdom and respect the creator of that wisdom. I suggest that the most loving thing you can do for yourself is respect yourself as the most beautiful creation of the most beautiful creator.

Separate for a moment what you have done from who you are in God. Take some time to define what you do that makes you respect yourself and others. At the end of this exercise you are going to have two lists. One is who I am in God. The other list is how I choose to behave. Remember the word who and how have the same letters just turned around. Both words are necessary to be a respectful human being.

Please remember to respect and value yourself. Sit down sometime this week and write out who you are in God and how you wish to demonstrate that.

Webster's Dictionary says Respect means "To consider worthy, of high regard." My question is who gets to decide worth? It is not me and it is not you. God already determined that we are worthy for we are respectfully and wonderfully made.

It is not ours to decide whether someone is worthy of Respect. The answer will always be the same—every creation of God is worthy of respect. We have the opportunity to make a decision about whether we can respect their actions, their Behaving. This brings us back to who and how. We must respect who people are; they are God's creation. We do not need to respect how they may behave. Mother Teresa told of her calling to be a servant to what the world would call unlovely, not worthy of high regard, the lepers, the poor and the needy. It came about when she realized this truth—Respect the WHO. She was on a crowded train in India. The smell, the sight of all those poor, dirty, sick people literally made her sick. She found herself judging them. And in that moment she realized that all of those souls were Christ in a distressing disguise. She came to respect with high regard each person no matter what they were disguised as.

Reasons to Go Within—Personal Application

Coaching Questions:

1. Do you believe the statement "You can't respect others if you can't respect yourself"?
2. What causes you to respect yourself?
3. What causes you to respect others?
4. Ponder the difference in Being and Behaving. How does this reflect on how you treat yourself and others?

Meditation

Close your eyes and take some long, slow breaths. Enter into your inner sanctuary of your heart. Send your breath into your heart chambers. As you step up to your Heart Throne, you are once again given a beautiful crown. You notice that the crown has beautiful jewels surrounding it. The first jewel is sparkling and dancing with light. It is the jewel of Trust. You know you can trust life because you can trust yourself and your God. You trust life just as you can trust your breath. You have a knowing that resonates from love. You notice the second jewel on your crown. It is full of radiant color. It is the jewel of Respect. In this moment you see so clearly who you are in God. You see your innocence, your beauty, your wonder. You see God in you. While looking into that jewel you also see God in every creation and creature on the planet. See God in the unlovely; the hurtful people for you know they are God's creation too! Affirm in this moment, I love and respect every Living Creature. I behold the light from the one source that is with all that is worthy of High Regard.

Namaste

The Jewel of Acceptance

What do you think of when you hear the word Acceptance? Acceptance is the third jewel in the crown that sits on the heart throne of love. The first thing that comes to my mind is surrender. There are two types of surrender. There is the white flag, toss in the towel kind of surrender and there is the type that provides relaxation. It allows us to relax like an infant in a parent's arms, knowing all of its needs are being handled by a loving, gentle parent. When this happens, all struggles and colicky feelings leave the body and the infant just melts into the parent's arms. The little one hears the soothing words, "It is ok, you are just fine, my sweet, sweet child."

Our loving creator can do that same thing for us when we are colicky and fearful. God whispers words of "Fear not for I am always with you, I have loved you with an everlasting love." This love is stronger than any outside event or person. You can relax now in the moment. I can surrender to "Thy will be done for I am One with thy will." Now that is on a <u>Good</u> Day!!

On a not so good day, it sounds more like this: "What the heck; didn't I already have this life lesson? Why are you making me repeat this assignment? I told you God, I accept you are in control, but I do not have to like it, do I? I do think I have some good ideas for how this should go. I had it under control. I guess I must accept that you are God and you will do what you think is best because after all, you are God!"

When this happens I am holding up the white flag of surrender, not the surrender that allows me to relax. This is the type of surrender that asks God to move quickly because we have made plans. We do not have time for this surrender. Both are accepting what is, but they are so very different. Aren't they? I believe the clearest prayer ever said about acceptance is the Serenity Prayer.

> God grant me the serenity to accept the things I cannot change
> The courage to change the things I can
> And the wisdom to know the difference.   *Reinhold Niebuhr*

Twenty seven words that hold the key to understanding the difference between acceptance and apathy, between a trusting surrender and I quit, between power and empowerment, between faith and fear. One of the secrets of love and acceptance is to relax, knowing the difference between external circumstances that are not going to change and the deeper understanding of the truth of our inner world of thought and mind action. We have been told we cannot control our feelings; however our thoughts create our feelings so our thoughts and actions influence greatly our emotions. This is where courage comes in.

Courage is not the absence of fear; it is what shows up when we are afraid. It is what causes us to speak up against injustice. It is the voice that says "I can make a difference." From Mary Anne Radmacher in *Courage Doesn't Always Roar*, "Sometimes it is a small voice that says I will do better tomorrow."

I often speak of one of my heroes Dr. Victor Frankl, who not only survived the Nazi concentration camps but used the experience to empower the world. In his book, *Man's Search for Meaning*, he concluded through research done during his incarceration that everything can be stripped from us in the external, but the last of human freedoms cannot. That freedom is the power to choose one's own attitude in any given situation. His land breaking work showed that the prisoners more likely to survive were those who found a sense of purpose even in the suffering. Frankl said it is a choice, a choice that takes courage and acceptance. It is the acceptance of what can and cannot be changed. To do that, wisdom is required. Our dignity can never be stripped away as clothes on our back because it comes from within.

> God grant me the serenity to accept the things I cannot change
> The courage to changes the things I can;
> And the wisdom to know the difference.   *Reinhold Niebuhr*

Courage does not always roar, sometimes it is a small voice that says I will do better tomorrow. Acceptance does not always make sense, but it feels right inside, it is the melting into the arms, with assurance that all is well. Wisdom is going within to find the answers. Serenity is the peace that comes from knowing all is well, even when the outside situations are appearing to the contrary. Acceptance is allowing the Infinite to move freely in your being. It is the knowing that there is a Divine Presence in you that wants your highest; I call it Spirit.

Surrender and Acceptance go together like Trust and Faith, like Love and Respect. Courage and Acceptance also go hand in hand. Wisdom calls forth acceptance and all leads to serenity. This all takes courage.

Acceptance is having the willingness to embrace the fullness of a situation or experience. It is an inner realization that all is well, regardless of the outward impression. If we do not practice acceptance we will never know Peace and Serenity. I once heard someone say that acceptance is knowing that there will be bugs at your picnic but you do not have to turn your whole lunch over to them.

When I come to acceptance of a situation then I am empowered to make conscious choices. Acceptance requires that I trust myself and God. Acceptance of the situation allows me to access the situation without resistance. I then can use my wisdom to know what I can and cannot do. This is where observation and discernment can help us separate the two. What is mine to do and what is not? Byron Katie, author of *Loving What Is!* poses four questions to help us with the discernment process.

1. Is it the truth? Facts
2. Can you absolutely know that it is true?
3. How do you react? What happens within you when you believe that story?
4. Where would you be without that thought?

These are good questions to help in the discernment process. The answers provide the wisdom to know the difference.

I also believe acceptance comes when we are in the present moment. Buddhists call it Mindfulness. Christian scripture says: "Take no thought for tomorrow, for tomorrow will take care of itself."

When we spend too much time with our thoughts of the past, we will lean toward depression because we are powerless about what was. When we spend too much time in the future, anxiety can happen because we cannot be sure of what will happen. We are powerless again. Ralph Waldo Emerson said: "With the past, I have nothing to do, nor with the future, so I LIVE NOW."

Abraham Maslow said: "The ability to be in the present moment is a major component of mental wellness."

Buddha said: "The secret of health for both mind and body is not to mourn the past, or worry about the future or anticipate troubles, but to live in the present moment wisely and earnestly."

God grant me the serenity to accept the things I cannot change
The courage to change the things I can;
And the wisdom to know the difference.   *Reinhold Niebuhr*

Staying in the present is easier when we focus our attention on appreciation and gratefulness. We all want serenity. Serenity comes from accepting what is not ours to change. It also comes when we ask the tough questions and see the truth! This is when we can surrender into acceptance.

What is it in your life that you may need to surrender? What is it that is keeping you from melting into the arms of the Infinite, most loving creator, allowing the peace that passes all understanding to run through your being like a stream of pure, refreshing water, bathing you in serenity? What is getting in the way? If it is a thought or a repeated story, ask the discerning questions. Is it true? Do you absolutely, 100% know it is true? What happens when you choose to believe this story? Can you imagine what you/your life would be like without the thought or story?

Many of our thoughts and stories are <u>not</u> 100% the truth and they do not serve us well. They do not lead to serenity but to confusion, a lack of clarity and assumptions which often causes anxiety.

Whatever it is that you need to surrender, whatever it is you need to accept to have serenity in your life, know that the truth does set us free, even when we may not like the truth. Knowing it, accepting it and deciding if it is yours to change is freedom. Serenity comes when you are in that place where you are able to know love, feel love and share love. You get rid of things that get in the way of love.

God grant me the serenity to accept the things I cannot change
The courage to change the things I can;
And the wisdom to know the difference.   *Reinhold Niebuhr*

Reasons to Go Within—Personal Application

Coaching Questions:

1. Can you remember a time when you white flag surrendered?
2. Can you remember when you "Relaxed in the arms of accepting surrender?" After recalling both, what made the difference between choosing one or the other?
3. How can you apply the Serenity Prayer more effectively in your life?

Meditation

Close your eyes, take some long, slow breaths. This is a time to go within to your heart sanctuary. Send your breath into your heart. As you step up to your Heart Throne, you are once again given a beautiful crown. You notice that the beautiful jewels are sparkling and dancing with light. You notice the jewel of trust; your eyes catch the light of the jewel of respect. A new jewel is present on your crown and it is the jewel of acceptance. This jewel allows you to enter the chamber of the heart called serenity. You must pass through the door of acceptance. You accept the good, the loving, and the beauty that is. You accept you are right where you need to be. You accept that all others are where they need to be. You accept what is not yours to change. You accept what is yours and you acknowledge that you have the courage and wisdom to do so.

And so it is.

The Jewel of Responsibility

We have placed the jewels of Trust, Respect and Acceptance on our crown that sits on the throne of our heart. We learned that Trust and Faith are synonymous. When we trust in ourselves and our God then we will not need to be so fearful of whether we can trust another. The second jewel is Respect. We were reminded that if we respect ourselves and others, love is present. Seeing the Christ nature in everyone no matter their disguise is essential to respecting ourselves. Seeing God as God is, a loving, compassionate force that is very proud of its creation. It is who we are. It is our being. It is how we behave. It is our actions. When our actions are congruent with who we are in our integrities, we will have self-respect. The third jewel is Acceptance. Acceptance is knowing what is not ours to change. We called on the prayer of Serenity to explain Acceptance.

> God grant me the serenity to accept the things I cannot change
> The courage to change the things I can;
> And the wisdom to know the difference.   *Reinhold Niebuhr*

We are reminded of the importance of living in this moment, to live in appreciation and gratitude for all that is. The way we can discern whether something is ours to change can be made clearer by asking the following questions: Is that thought that I am having the truth? Am I 100%, absolutely sure it is the truth? How do I feel when I have that thought? What would it be like for me right now if I did not?

This is the last Reasoning in the series on Matters of the Heart and it is the jewel of Responsibility.

I want to share a rather radical thought when it comes to Responsibility and relationships. We have been told that in any relationship each party needs to give 50% (50/50). Then we advanced our thinking to the idea that each of us must give 100% (100/100). The problem with both of these concepts is when one decides that the other is not giving their share, a break down occurs. In other words, this concept comes with an expectation with another. When my expectations are not met, I somehow think my part in the contract is now void and I have a right to no longer give my 100%.

In the 100/0 Principle, there are no expectations that are not met because I own my part 100%. The 100/0 Principle asks that each of us take full responsibility for our part in all our relationships. That is 100%. Expect nothing is the 0. The paradox of this principle is you will receive benefits beyond any expectation you could have had. There are no guarantees, but the majority of the time this principle works.

Yes, it can be uncomfortable to live this way because it goes against our beliefs and teachings. Jack Canfield, the co-author of *The Chicken Soup for the Soul Series* says: "If we are not a little uncomfortable every day, we are not growing. All the good stuff is just outside our comfort zone."

My disclaimer to the 100/0 Principle is in situations that involve integrity; lying, betraying and/or abuse. Of course you should not stay or give 100% to a violation of integrity. This is where boundaries become extremely important. It is your responsibility to not allow another to step over your boundaries. Do not expect others to be responsible for what is yours. You must care for your own well-being. This is ours, 100%. But the paradox is that people will and do care about your being. The 100% is about 100% kindness. 100% respect. 100% gratitude. 100% graciousness. 100% persistence in living in your integrity.

Can you imagine for a moment a world where everyone knows the truth and power of this principle? Imagine a world in which everyone gave 100% and respected 100%. Well as John Lennon put it, "Imagine a world of only love." That is what it would take to have the world he sang about. It would take everyone choosing not to blame, not to judge, not to disrespect and not to victimize anyone. It means we would all take responsibility for peace, for compassion, for a better world and better relationships. "You may say that I am a dreamer, but I am not the only one," John Lennon

When I first heard about this principle, I was a little taken back, yet very intrigued. I realized on my good days, this is how I live my life and it works. On the not so good days it is clear that I hold back, give only 60% and expect someone else to give the other 40%. I then find myself disappointed when others do not contribute at the level of my expectations. Please do not misunderstand me; I am not suggesting that we are responsible for another's happiness or even their whims. But I am 100% responsible for how I choose to react. I am 100% responsible for the way I treat people. This includes how I show up on the job, and how I show up with my family and with my friends. This is what I call Authentic Responsibility. It is not about duty, it is about dignity. It is about being 100% and then making a 100% difference in the world. Gandhi reminded us to "Be the change you want to see in the world."

Speaking for myself because that is the only person I can speak for, I can say I am 100% responsible for my spiritual condition. I am 100% responsible for respecting you, for accepting what is, for trusting others and my God. President Kennedy said "Ask not what your country can do for you; ask what you can do for your country." That is the 100/0 Principle.

Commitment is demonstrated in actions. Love is demonstrated in actions, in acts of love. It is demonstrated in giving back. Ask yourself what is it that you can give to promote growth in you and others. As we grow and learn, we need to promote and support more people who give 100% for something they can believe in. Where can you promote this growth in others?

I have learned that I grow in spirit in the direct proportion to my willingness to give, to serve without any expectation of getting something in return. Giving for the sheer JOY of it! It is true, give 100/0 and your life will be richer than you could ever imagine. Ask not what others can do for you; ask what you can do for others. The responsibility of LOVE is to be you in all your magnificence 100%!

Reasons to Go Within—Personal Application

Coaching Questions:

1. What are your thoughts on the 100% to 0% principle?
2. Where does the principle not apply for you? (What are your boundaries?)
3. John Lennon's words say "Imagine a world that is filled with acceptance." How do you think the world would look if everyone accepted responsibility for their words, actions and deeds 100%?

Meditation:

Close your eyes, take some deep, slow breaths. Imagine a world where everyone understands and lives the 100/0 Principle. You get up in the morning, go to your place of employment and everyone is giving 100%. You come home and everyone in the family takes responsibility for respecting, loving and giving, without expectation.

Imagine a world where each nation is living this principle. Imagine. Imagine.

It can begin right here, right now with you and me! "You may say I am a dreamer but I am not the only one." Join me, and the world can be one.

And so it is!

The Soul's Longing for Intimacy

I would imagine that there is not a reader of this material who has NOT longed for a close connection to another human being. Webster's definition of the word Intimacy is: "A close connection."

Let's begin by looking at close encounters. A close encounter of the first kind is an encounter that longs to be connected to another outside of our self. In this quest for Intimacy, we find the love of a lover, love of friends, love of family and love of pets.

A close encounter of the second kind is the encounter with the longing to be connected to our self. It is to know oneself, to enjoy the company of our self. It is to care for and nurture one's self. It is to know one's purpose and unique intentions. It is to know one's sacred contract.

A close encounter of the third kind is the encounter with our Creator, our beloved. It is the most sacred of all encounters. It is mysterious and mystical. It is the twin hearts of human and divine beating as one, two sparks burning as one flame where Spirit and Soul meet. This intimacy cannot be damaged or destroyed. It is the deepest. It is the highest form of intimacy.

Because of our humanness we desire all three encounters with intimacy, human, our self and our Creator. We were created to be in connection and in community with others and God.

We are pack animals, if you will. Some of us are a little more extroverted than others, just as in the animal kingdom; nevertheless, it has been statically proven that we thrive much better in community. In the creation story in Genesis 2:18, "And the lord God said, It is not good that man is alone, I will make him a help meet." So even the Creator of all tried the alone thing only to find it was NOT good. God did not want to be alone. Man did not do well alone. God saw that man did not do well alone. God saw that an improvement was needed, so God created woman—this by the way is my interpretation of that scripture.

Just as I imagined that there is not a person who has not longed for connection. There probably is not a person who has not felt hurt because of a close connection of the first kind with another human being. The more we expose ourselves, allow ourselves to become intimately involved, the more potential there is for hurt.

What are we supposed to do? The more we get involved and get connected, the more potential there is for hurt AND the great truth is the soul's journey and longing is to be connected. How do we manage this?

Do we give up the soul's calling just to avoid being hurt? Is that even possible if it comes from deep in our core? Just the process of giving up the soul's longing for connectedness feels hurtful, a loss.

Intimacy must embrace the possibility of hurt and vulnerability. "It is better to have loved and lost than to never have loved at all," Alfred Lord Tennyson. My definition of vulnerable is: ULTIMATE TRUST IN GOD'S DIVINE PLAN. There have been many times on this life journey that I have opened up to another I am connected to and it has led to being hurt. I can recall multiple times saying "I am done." I promised myself that I am never going to let myself get that close to another. I promised myself that I would flee before I could be hurt.

Yet, after the pain, the disappointment subsides and I come to a place of healing. My defenses go down and before you know it I am volunteering my heart for another mission connection. What keeps us coming back for more? What keeps us wanting to be connected?

I believe it is because our soul longs for it. That is what brought us here. We are here to be connected! This longing is so great that we are willing to keep risking, taking that chance. Relationships create risks.

The more involvement we have, the greater potential for growth, connection and love. Yet with that potential comes the greater risk of hurt. Maybe that is why some of us are more willing to have intimate relationships with our animals rather than take the risk with people. Animals (unless extremely fearful) are very predictable. Most of us who have furry companions know just what to expect from them. NOT SO MUCH IN THE HUMAN WORLD. I know where to go when I need a loving touch, a look that says that I am wonderful, a walk or a good cuddle. I go to my dog and cats and I am seldom disappointed. I am safe.

Very few of us can say the same with as much reliability in regard to our human connections. As our distrust in this society climbs, so does our soul's longing for connection. Maybe that is why the pet industry is booming. There is an abundance of pet clothes, pet products, pet care and pet stores. Maybe this is because we are turning more to the animal community and to a connection we know we can trust, a connection that will not judge, betray, hurt or disappoint us.

Yet, what do you think our future holds if the fear of risk and involvement continues to grow? What if it becomes safer to be disconnected than it does to be involved? What if we are no longer willing to put ourselves out there? What is the answer? Our soul needs connection, yet connection often opens us up for potentially being hurt and rejected. If we deny our soul's longing we can end up lonely and empty. If we follow the soul's longing we must become vulnerable. Remember my definition of vulnerable—ULTIMATE TRUST IN GOD'S PROTECTION AND DIVINE PLAN.

In *The New Earth*, Eckhart Tolle speaks of the emergence of a new earth, similar to what is referred to in the Bible, Isaiah 65:17. "For, behold, I create new heavens and a new earth: and the former shall not be remembered, nor come to mind." Revelations 21:1, "And I saw a new heaven and a new earth: for the first heaven and the first earth were passed away and there was no more sea." Eckhart Tolle says for this to happen we must let go of what he calls "ego." Now for Tolle ego is anything that gives the illusion of disconnection or me-ness. It is deeply connected to the past, conditioned by the past. Ego comes from fear. Thus the soul's great longing for intimacy is quenched. Ego is fear. God is Love. Ego is me-ness. Spirit is oneness. Ego is alone. God and Spirit are community.

Fear is not reality because it is a projection. Think of it, when you say you are afraid of something, it is not currently happening. An example would be the following: I say that I am afraid of bankruptcy, when it is obvious that I am not bankrupt. This is a projection which means it is not real. If I were bankrupt I would say "I am bankrupt," I would not say I am afraid of bankruptcy.

A Course in Miracles gives us great insight. What if everything is either Love or Fear? What is Real is LOVE. The Soul's longing is for Love, and Love cannot exist without an object to Love. Love serves no purpose if it is not directed toward something or someone.

Love is in the now. Love is Energy. You can never get too much love. There in is truth; it is not a projection or an illusion. Now I ask, "What is our future if we become full of fear? What would our future look like if we become full of love, community and connectedness? What if there was an intimacy with others, an intimacy with ourselves, an intimacy with this planet and with our God?" There would be no environmental breakdown, no hunger and no destruction. There would be no prejudice or violence. There would be no wars.

In every encounter we have, we have the opportunity to cultivate love. Relationships are here to quicken our connection to our spirit, the beloved sacred energy of all things. *A Course in Miracles* says "Everyone we meet will either be our savior or our crucifier depending on what we choose; "it will not be of their choosing, but of our own. Whatever we focus on regarding the story, whatever we tell about our self, about them and the purpose of the encounter will determine the outcome.

Remember connection through relationships is God's way of moving us along through the enlightened process. It is Spirit's plan, to lead the soul to greater awareness and Love. In connection we are given an opportunity to open up the potential for Love and release the illusion of fear. Perfect love casts out fear.

May I suggest: We consider love over fear. We choose community over non-involvement. We choose vulnerability over isolation. May we risk; so our dreams, visions, encounters lead us to love and fulfill our soul's longing for closeness, connectedness.

Meditation:

In your safe place you go. Here you are vulnerable, there are NO RISKS for this is where Spirit dwells. You have come to this place for a glimpse of The New Earth. You have a knowing that is upon us and you have been chosen to be part of its unveiling. You quiver with excitement as you await the debut.

You see before you a world of beauty. It is a world of PEACE. You notice that the Peace is coming from within you radiating out. Wherever you are PEACE radiates out to all of those around you.

Then you hear these words: "And now I will show you the most excellent way." And behold, I have created a new heaven and a new earth. The former things will be remembered no more, nor come to mind. Love is the more excellent way.

And so it is!

I Corinthians 13, Love Story

We all love a good love story don't we? Even when we are watching a love story on a screen or reading it in a book, we can become the characters; we feel their pain and their ecstasy. It becomes so real, so true. We cry when they cry, laugh when they laugh. We even feel our life's energy being taken away if they are to die. Music, books and art all make attempts to portray the energy, the magnitude of a good love story.

Many times our human version of what love is and how it should behave does not match the reality of the situation. And when our expectation for love is not met we often blame the other person or ourselves, don't we? The real culprit is fear. When love does not turn out as we had hoped for, expected, longed for or invested in, know that fear is what blocked the energy of love in its highest form.

In Don Miguel Ruiz's book, *The Mastery of Love*, he speaks of the energy of love going in two tracks. The first track is Love which is highest energy and the second is Selfish Fear which is lower energy or selfish survival thinking.

Aspects mentioned in the *Mastery of Love* by Don Miguel Ruiz:

LOVE	FEAR
Love <u>wants</u> to do things	Fear <u>has</u> to do things
Love limits its expectations, sees only possibilities—Does not take things personally—Does not harbor resentment	Fear is Full of Expectations and often brings disappointment. Fear blames others
Love is not controlling—it sees that others have their own answers. Love supports everyone in their quest to find their answers.	Fear tries to control and make choices for others. Fear doesn't allow us to make our own choices
Love respects oneself and others	Fear has no respect, it is only fear
Love is generous, love gives to self and others	Fear is selfish, "It's ALL ABOUT ME"
Love is honest; living authentically	Fear is dishonest, not telling yourself and others the truth
Love forgives and lets go	Fear gives punishment, it makes you and others pay again and again

I want to thank my dear friend Linda for teaching me this content.

Many of us know the beautiful words written in the Bible in the first book of Corinthians 13 "Though I speak with the tongues of men and of angels, but have not love, I have become sounding brass or a clanging cymbal. And though I have *the gift of* prophecy, and understand all mysteries and all knowledge, and though I have all faith, so that I could remove mountains, but have not love, I am nothing. And though I bestow all my goods to feed *the poor,* and though I give my body to be burned, but have not love, it profits me nothing. Love suffers long *and* is kind; love does not envy; love does not parade itself, is not puffed up; does not behave rudely, does not seek its own, is not provoked, thinks no evil; does not rejoice in iniquity, but rejoices in the truth; bears all things, believes all things, hopes all things, endures all things. Love never fails. But whether *there are* prophecies, they will fail; whether *there are* tongues, they will cease; whether *there is* knowledge, it will vanish away. For we know in part and we prophesy in part. But when that which is perfect has come, then that which is in part will be done away. When I was a child, I spoke as a child, I understood as a child, I thought as a child; but when I became a man, I put away childish things. For now we see in a mirror, dimly, but then face to face. Now I know in part, but then I shall know just as I also am known. And now abide faith, hope, love, these three; but the greatest of these *is* love."

Often these words are read at weddings and ceremonies to renew vows. It is a perfect version of love without fear.

Perfection is seldom gained but is often sought after. Divine love is I Corinthians 13. Human love is the seeking after the perfection. Sometimes our seeking leads us to discouragement and even a cynical outlook. When we remember ours is to honor this highest of energy forms—LOVE, knowing there is but one perfect love, we can often rise to the occasion.

There is an ancient love story that is the perfect metaphor for human love and divine love coming together for a moment in time. It comes from the collection of King Arthur and his royal knights. This is from the Romantic Age. Sir Gawain, one of King Arthur's loyal knights agrees to marry Ragnell, a grotesquely unattractive woman in exchange for information that would save King Arthur's life. When Sir Gawain's wedding night came, instead of the town celebrating the handsome, brave knight's wedding, they were sad, feeling somehow that this situation was not fair. It was not how love stories are supposed to go. It did not fit their belief system about perfect love!

On his wedding night, Sir Gawain waited for his bride, Ragnell in his bedroom chamber. The room was dimly lit, the door opened, Ragnell climbed into bed next to him and lay beside him. She said, "You have kept your promise and much more. You have never shown me pity or revulsion. All I ask of you is one kiss, you need to never give me more." Sir Gawain did not hesitate and lovingly leaned over and kissed her. Before his eyes, Ragnell turned into a beautiful woman. Startled, he jumped from his bed and asked "Who are you? Where is my wife?" She said, "I am your wife, I am Ragnell." She then began to tell him her story. You see, her naughty stepbrother, Gromer was always jealous and resentful because she was so beautiful, so loved by all. And if that weren't enough, she would not follow his commands just because he was a man. Gromer went to his even naughtier mother, the Queen, who also was jealous of Ragnell. The Queen turned Ragnell into a most unattractive pitied woman.

The second part of the story teaches that only selfless love could free her of the curse. She explained to Sir Gawain, "Since you treated me with that type of love, you now have a choice to make. I can be a beautiful wife by day so all will admire you and believe you to be one of the luckiest men and you can be proud. But, at night when we lie next to each other I will be ugly again. Or I could be ugly Ragnell all day and people will pity you. But at night I will be beautiful. Which do you prefer?"

Without hesitation, Sir Gawain said, "This should not be my choice, it is yours. You must choose for yourself. I will accept either decision as long as it is your will."

With that response, the curse was lifted and Ragnell was beautiful day and night. This is a GREAT story of human love and sacred love, is it not?

Humanly, this is a wonderful love story as:

- He was not concerned with his own desires
- He wanted what was best for her
- He saw beyond the physical and wanted only his partner's happiness and well being
- He wanted to empower her and that healed them both

From a Sacred, Divine, Love Story, Sir Gawain is a metaphor for our creator, God. God only wants our best and highest personal good. God only sees our beauty, no matter what physical form it comes in. God supports and allows us to make our own choices.

<u>God Is Love—Love Is God.</u>

God Is Not an EMOTION or <u>a Feeling</u>.

God is Perfect Love—No Fear Attached.

God—Love—is an act of endless forgiveness of self and others.

God—Love—is not a definition, it is a journey to the sacred, the Synchrodivinity of the creation of ONENESS.

Reasons to Go Within—Personal Application

Coaching Questions:

1. Examine more closely the table of love versus fear that was created from information provided in *Mastery of Love* by Don Miguel Ruiz. Which of these items are most difficult to demonstrate?
2. What was your favorite part of the love story of Ragnell and Sir Gawain?
3. Do you believe sacred love is not an emotion or feeling? If so, what makes God's love different than human love?

Meditation:

Breathe comfortably, lovingly. See a pink light coming from above your head moving through your body from your head to the soles of your feet. The soft pink light creates a blanket of protection that covers your whole being. You feel a warmth and an energy coming from your chest, right behind your heart. Right now—whisper to yourself: "I am love. I know the oneness of all creation." Breathe in This Truth of Being.

Whisper to yourself, "My love creates harmony in the world and in me. My love is the demonstration of the fullness of my soul." As you sit enfolded in the soft pink blanket of love, you hear a whisper coming from your heart. I am an energy of beauty and an energy of love. I am boundless in resources, I am only possibilities. My energy grows stronger as you open your heart to me. I will bring you more love and beauty. Your thankfulness and appreciation multiplies the good in your life. My nature is to give, allow my nature to give. Allow me to fulfill my nature in my interactions with you. I am love. Allow me to demonstrate my lovingness. It is your choice. Look for <u>my</u> love and you will find it. Having found my love, expect more of it. And So It Is!

Section III

Your Cosmic G.P.S.

Your Cosmic G.P.S. Introduction

A word I use often is Synchrodivinity. Synchrodivinity is a word my friend Johanna discovered for me. I was searching for a word that could describe those moments in our lives (which happen all the time) when you are in synch with the Divine. Johanna is often called a wordsmith. Synchrodivinity is one of her most precious finds.

Synchrodivinity is always present, it is always happening yet it is our own awareness that moves the energy field and assists us to create or understand its purpose. This then affirms the existence of a Divine presence involved in the creation of our lives.

There are always signs and symbols to help us find our way along with our internal guidance system (G.P.S. or God Positioning System). We have everything we need to get us where we need to go.

Synchrodivinity

"How great are his signs and how mighty are his wonders. His kingdom is an everlasting kingdom and his dominion is from generation to generation." Daniel 4:3

How many times in your life has something happened that you just chalked up to luck, good or bad, you chalked it up to coincidence? Many times we have a tendency to overlook the Destiny or the Divine piece of coincidences.

When we look at happenings and events in our lives from a coincidence perspective we can miss out on the Divine perspective. These are the lessons and blessings that are presenting themselves. For in the Synchro Divine world, all is connected. It is the ultimate oneness of the Universe. Synchrodivinity is our message from the universe.

The entire universe is connected, not just now, but we are connected to all that was and all that will be. Dr. Carl Jung, one of the fathers of modern psychology called one form of Synchrodivinity the collective unconscious. The thought is that there can be no coincidence or it just happened without rhyme, reason or purpose. It is all part of our Sacred Contract or Path. Our whole existence has purpose and is connected to the universal purpose and to Spiritual purpose. Some might call it Destiny. In other words we are here to fulfill our Purpose. And the Universe conspires and supports that journey; the unfolding comes up as Synchrodivinity.

Synchrodivinity is when you are in synch with the Divine. It is when you have a knowing that everything that has happened and is happening is for the purpose of Highest Consciousness. Synchrodivinity is always happening. It is our awareness that helps us evolve through events in our lives. In the book *The Alchemist*, Paulo Coelho calls this "Our Personal Legend." "Everyone comes here with a Personal Legend." In this book, the old man named Melchizedek is explaining his sacred contract, speaking to the young shepherd boy who is about to go on a journey to the pyramids to discover his treasure, his Personal Legend.

From *The Alchemist*: *"I'm the King of Salem," the old man had said.*

"Why would a king be talking with a shepherd?" the boy asked, awed and embarrassed.

"For several reasons. But let's say that the most important is that you have succeeded in discovering your Personal Legend."

The boy didn't know what a person's Personal Legend was.

"It's what you have always wanted to accomplish. Everyone, when they are young, knows what their Personal Legend is. At that point in their lives, everything is clear and everything is possible. They are not afraid to dream, and to yearn for everything they would like to see happen to them in their lives. But, as time passes, a mysterious force begins to convince them that it will be impossible for them to realize their Personal Legend."

. . . "It's a force that appears to be negative, but actually shows you how to realize your Personal Legend. It prepares your spirit and your will, because there is one great truth on this planet: whoever you are, or whatever you are, or whatever it is that you do, when you really want something, it's because that desire originated in the soul of the universe. It's your mission on earth."

. . . *"To realize one's Personal Legend is a person's only real obligation. All things are one. And, when you want something, all the universe conspires in helping you to achieve it."*

Melchizedek has deep spiritual meaning. It comes from Genesis 14:18 which says, "And Melchizedek, King of Salem brought forth bread and wine and was the priest of the most high God."

He is considered an archetype of Christ. Similarly, we are archetypes of the Christ.

The order of Melchizedek refers to the King of Peace, a priesthood that has no end. It is the Most High, possessor of heaven and earth. Metaphorically this is our Destiny, Our Sacred Contract, it is the order of Melchizedek. We are the possessors of heaven and earth. Melchizedek earlier had told the boy why people give up their Personal Legends, their dreams. He said it is because people often believe the world's greatest lie. Do you know what that is? Do you <u>want</u> to know what that is?

It is this: "At a certain point in our lives, we lose control of what is happening to us and we come to believe our lives are controlled by fate 'or coincidence'." That is a BIG LIE! Do not believe the lie that we are controlled by random circumstances and we have no control. According to Melchizedek in order to find your treasure, to Live Your Legend, we must follow omens, signs. God has prepared a path for each to follow. You just have to read the omens God has left for you. If we push forward impulsively, we may fail to see the signs and omens left by God along our path. Those signs and omens are Synchrodivinity.

Biblical References to Signs

I Samuel 10:7—"And let it be when these signs are come unto thee, that thou do as occasion serve thee for God is with thee."

I Samuel 10:9—"And it was so, that when he had turned his back to go from Samuel, God gave him another heart: and all those signs came to pass that day."

Exodus 10 1,2—"The Lord told Moses, Go to Pharaoh, and show him my signs. That thou mayest tell in the ears of his son's son, what things I have wrought in Egypt, and my signs which I have done among them: that they may know I am the Lord."

Isaiah 8:18—"Behold, I and the children whom the Lord hath given me, are signs and for wonders in Israel from the Lord of hosts which dwell in the land of Zion."

Acts 2:22—". . . Hear these words: Jesus of Nazareth, a man approved of God among you by miracles and wonders and signs which God did by him in the midst of you as ye yourselves also know."

John 20:30—"And many signs truly did Jesus in the presence of his disciples which are not written in this book, yet those that are written are that you might believe."

To fully grasp Synchrodivinity we must understand and acknowledge the Nature of Being. The I AM that aligns with what is happening on your earthly path. This means to be willing, open to seeing all that is before you, to be open to see it with curiosity and wonder, to explore the meanings. When we are in synch with The Divine, we are allowing our conscious mind to connect with Divine Mind and that is where all possibilities unfold. All dreams begin from Divine Mind.

The Alchemist is suggesting that we pay attention to the Divine Synchronicities in our life. It suggests we pay attention to the signs throughout our lives.

There is remedial learning and then there is higher learning. When living from Synchrodivinity our perspective looks for the deeper meaning around us and does not look at things from a fatalistic view. We choose to see all the possibilities of the Universe.

Synchrodivinity is to be less invested in the Whys and more interested in the How and the What questions. How does this reflect my purpose? What does this mean? What could this mean as it supports my Divinity? Or, how is God using this right now to open me up to new possibilities?

Synchrodivinity comes through people, places and events that your soul attracts into your life to assist in your evolution into higher consciousness, your Sacred Contract, your Personal Legend.

The more consciously aware and open we are to Synchrodivinity, the higher vibrational frequency we put out. We are turning up the voltage, the Power. The Power is of Divine Energy. I suggest that for this next week, be even more aware of the signs and omens of Divine Directions. Do not be afraid to ask for direction and signs leading you to your Personal Legend.

Signs can come in words, people, dreams, omens, déjà vues, creative ideas, intuitions, animals, objects and aha moments. All that you need to know is already here waiting for you to see. If you are fearful about finances, ask for a sign of prosperity and abundance. If you are fearful about physical safety, pray and affirm protection and then ask for a sign to know what is safe. Whatever it is, ask for signs and be willing to see it.

Reasons to Go Within—Personal Application

Coaching Questions:

1. Do you believe in Synchrodivinity? If so, how do you explain it?
2. Think of times in your life when you have experienced it. What was the outcome?
3. What is your "Personal Legend"?

Mistake Proof Meditation

Find a comfortable position in your chair, hands on your lap, and feet flat on the floor. Close your eyes and take three gentle breaths, inhaling through the nose, and exhaling through the mouth . . . Continue breathing gently with your mouth closed. As you do, feel a wave of relaxation moving from the top of your head, slowly down, down, down to the tips of your toes . . . Breathe gently and tell yourself that you are safe and divinely protected . . . Know that all you do is guided by a loving energy that will assist you in all your needs and lead you to your ultimate joy . . . Release feelings of suspicion or doubt in your ability to communicate with the Universe, and tell yourself you will welcome all messages/signs that come to you in a kind and loving way . . . As you continue to breathe gently, inhale peace and tranquility and exhale all doubt and fear. You are a child of the Universe and it is here to help you now. Welcome it . . . Relax in this moment of peace for a bit . . . Take another gentle breath, and as you exhale ask the Universe, Creator, God a question and affirm that you will look for signs that lead you to the answer. Maybe may want to play with God. If so, pick something that you will use as a sign of God's presence and guidance. This may be a color, it may be an animal or it could be an object. Then notice each time it shows up. Remember to look for it. We get what we look for when it shows up. Thank God.

Sacred Signs Symbols, Synchronicity

Since the beginning of the beginning, we have been seeking to Know God. We know within our very being we have the ability to communicate with God. We pray, we meditate, we talk to the Divine. We talk, and we talk, did I say we talk. Yet listening, hearing, seeing God's answers and communication to us is not so familiar. Finding the answers is often a bit of a mystery. I find it interesting we will ask for guidance, and we will pray for answers but then miss the message when it comes. I wonder how many times we were given the answer but we did not see it or understand it. The universe wants us to receive the guidance we need. Because of this truth I believe that there are <u>always</u> answers to our questions. The answers often do not come in verbal cues and language (words). Dr. Carl Jung believed that the way to remove the barriers that language imposes on us when connecting with divine guidance is through symbolism. Symbols connect to that which cannot be expressed in words. Do you <u>really</u> believe that the INFINITE speaks through words? Think about it!

Well, even if we do believe that God speaks through language, there is so much evidence that says that guidance does come from symbols, signs, angels, guides, nature and intuition.

A Sacred Sign is a message from the Spirit world to the human world. The language of Spirit <u>can</u> come in words. I believe the way this happens is that it first starts with an energy, a vibration and then it is channeled into words. Verbiage is Spirit's second language. Signs and Symbols are Gods native or original tongue. "Be still and know that I AM!" Often we are the interrupters. Guidance can come from angels, spirit guides and loved ones who have crossed over. The communication from these special messengers will often use words from the other side, channeling or interpreting the language of Spirit so that we may understand it.

Because we are here to be the hands, the voice of God on earth, we can bring messages and guidance. Have you ever just felt led to call someone or pray for someone without knowing why? And then find out they had needed the very thing, you were guided to do.

Since the recorded history of the human race, we have been seeking and finding guidance from signs and symbols. There are some universal symbols that are considered the most ancient. They are the circle, often represented in mandalas, medicine wheels and labyrinths. There is the spiral circle which can represent gratitude and eternity. There is the Interlocking Triangles (Star of David) symbolizing "AS ABOVE SO BELOW."

Ancient sacred symbols contain a universal cosmic wisdom that can be a powerful tool of guidance. By honoring them we gain access to amazing sacred resources that guide us. What I want to convey and hopefully encourage you to do is open yourself up to the idea of allowing guidance and direction to come through signs that are always present though God's original language.

We were not sent to Earth School without teachers. Every school has teachers and just like any classroom experience if we fail to do our work, or don't pay attention to our teachers, the lessons gets harder and the experience is not so fun. When exam time comes, we will not know the answers.

Dr. Carl Jung coined the term synchronicity to explain signs and events, these events are messages that go deeper than coincidences. Synchrodivinity means that times and signs are divine messages and guidance to help us. Again, I thank my spiritual sister Johanna for finding that term and believing with me in Synchrodivinity.

It is often the method the universe uses to give us answers or direction. It is Synchrodivinity! We ask for signs, put out the intention, invoke the energy through our emotions; it is how we manifest. But can you imagine saying I want to see something and then close your eyes? Well, that is what many of us do when we pray or ask for an answer and then fail to look for the signs. Often we interpret the signs that do come to us based on what we want in our fixed mindset, rather than being open to all possibilities. Know that the signs are Divine guidance and will not lead us astray, but we must give up our own agenda to be guided by the signs.

This week I want you to play with the universe a bit. Ask for something, a sign to a question you have been seeking and then look (eyes open) for the answers. While doing this remember signs can be very subtle or in techno color and surround sound. I think that the signs come in different levels because of where we are in our trusting, our knowing, and our belief in the source. By being allowed to be directed by signs we are exercising our faith muscles, so following signs not only gives us direction but it increases our faith. Anything we want to be good at, we must practice right?

Another teacher of signs, Adrian Calabrese, teaches that we can discern signs if we practice what she calls "Keys to the Knowledge of the Universe." Those keys are broken down into three steps. ASK, ACCEPT and TRUST. Interestingly, those are the steps used in manifesting by all successful manifestors, creators. That is what the word manifest means to me, to create. We are co-creators meaning we are creating with God. Spirit Space was created from an idea that came from signs that said Go—Green light—Yes! Then we all became co-manifestors with God. We did not create Spirit Space.

God was the energy, the CEO and we all joined the team. The term we use for this is co-creating. The first key is to ASK.

Key # 1—Ask

Some find it difficult to ask for things. Some find it difficult to seek guidance from fellow earth students, let alone from God. Sometimes asking is difficult because we do not believe we deserve to receive. I get a little weary of hearing advanced earth students playing this card. There is no such thing as deserving or undeserving. There is no deserving or underserving principle but there is a reap what you sow, karmic principle.

If you are here and you have a dream, you are automatically in the Yes Club, just by the nature of the Being. It is not You that makes You a member of the Yes Club, it is the Creator who created you that endowed us high-priority status, Gold Club membership. God respects everyone; God will talk to ANYONE, ANYTIME because that is who God IS! There is no undeserving.

Another problem that often arises with the key of ASKING is "I do not know what to ask for." That often is because you do not know what you REALLY want or you are afraid that if you got it you would not know what to do with it. ASK anyways. The universe will help you sort it all out. The universe will give you what it will take to make it happen or NOT. When it does not happen, that can be as strong a sign as having something happen.

Key #2—Accept

Well, asking is one thing, accepting or receiving is another class. Biblical scripture says "ASK and you shall RECEIVE." Always it is your choice as to whether you receive it. Life is like a dessert tray. God is always passing it, you can look and say "Oh that looks so good," but not take anything offered. You may worry about the calories, but just know it will come by again and again. You will get many opportunities to partake and accept or not. Each time the dessert tray of life is passed, there are some favorite standbys and then the Creator Pastry Chef will put a new tempting morsel on the tray. I wonder how many of God's desserts you have passed up because you were afraid of the calories or you were just too full of other things. Think about it? The tray will come by again but maybe not with the same goodies!

Key #3—Trust

For many who have been taught the censored version of the Judeo Christian life, trusting signs is sometimes a challenge. I said censored because the uncensored version spoke of signs, symbols and miracles all of the time! The uncensored version includes Gnostic gospels and sacred writings that were not allowed in our present version of the Bible.

Guidance comes from nature, animals, stones, numbers, stars, channeling, dreams and our own GPS (God Positioning System, intuition) in the uncensored version. So Trust asks us to abandon our conditional way of thinking. It asks us to transition to a more universal, all inclusive way of perception. It means having the knowing that we were not expected to go to Earth School without teachers. We are so deeply loved, supported, respected that there is no way The Master teacher would ever leave us floundering, not knowing what to do.

Are you ready to play with the universe this week and maybe the rest of your life by seeking answers through signs, symbols and Synchrodivinity? Remember it can come through animal symbols, nature, crystals and stones, numbers, dreams and Synchrodivinity. It can come from our intuition, our GPS. Do not forget the five senses. What you see, what you hear—reality signs as I call them are important in order for the three keys to work.

ASK, ACCEPT, TRUST—We need to agree to not allow fear to be a sign. Many times I have not received the dessert because I was afraid. I convinced myself that it was God telling me NO. Our God is a YES God. It is good to have people around to remind us of the truth when fear tries to creep in. I have been blessed with friends who do that for me. It often comes in the form of a question such as "What if God is not telling you no?"

I do acknowledge and respect that there are healthy fears that help to keep us safe, but there are fears that will limit us if we don't face them.

Georgia O'Keefe said "I have been afraid every day of my life and I never let it stop me from doing what I really wanted to do."

Many times we believe fear comes from God. Certain fears come from a primal survival instinct to keep us safe and alive. God did not give us a Spirit of Fear regarding decisions about growth, direction and creation. May it be said that fear is not our guide, maybe a protector, but not our guide. We are often at a fork in the road on our way to the Emerald City and we must proceed. Healthy fear can give us wisdom as to how to get to the Emerald City. Unhealthy fear can cause us to fall asleep in the poppy fields.

Reasons to Go Within—Personal Application

Coaching Questions:

1. How do you hear God speak to you?
2. What makes it hard to receive a message from God?
3. What do you believe about fear?
4. How has fear stopped you from doing something you wanted to do? Was it healthy fear or unhealthy fear?
5. What would you do if you knew you could not fail?
6. Name 3 friends who remind you of who you are and who God is?

Meditation

Close your eyes, get comfortable in your chairs, place your hands in a receiving position, and take three gentle breaths. As you do this notice the wave of relaxation moving from the top of your head, slowly down, down, down, to the tips of your toes. Breathing gently, be aware of each breath. Tell yourself you are ready to begin a week long dialogue with the universe. Feel how wonderful that thought is. Experience the joy that you and all of creation will be by communing, discovering, learning, finding direction as co-creators. Now give thanks for the experience of earth school, the opportunity to meet your new teachers who have come to support and guide you. If you are willing, make a promise to yourself to remain open to divine guidance and receive the messages. And so it is!

Synchrodivinity—Is Your Synchro-Destiny

Earlier I presented Synchrodivinity and I think it bears revisiting. What is it that you believe about coincidences? What do you make of having a Sacred Contract with the Infinite? Do you know yours? Do you believe in Destiny? Do you think everything that happens is for a reason? Do you think that everything is part of a plan that is bigger than that moment? These are important questions. The answers to these questions will determine how you show up in life.

I believe that we are all here as part of an Infinite plan and everything happens for a reason. We all have choices that can lead us to different outcomes and destinations. I show up fully engaged in my Destiny because of this belief. How does one know what their Destiny is? And how can one support the journey with clarity, ease and grace if we don't believe in a Destiny?

A few years ago, these questions led me to seek a better understanding of Synchrodivinity. I know that in the Questions of Life, there lie the answers. I also know that no one has <u>your</u> answers. I am here to support the <u>wisdom that lies within your soul</u>. We are seekers. Seekers do not look for dogma for as soon as there is "the way," there is no need to seek. Spirit Space is the home of the seeker. It is the place for those looking for the answers to the questions that are only found from within. Not everyone who stops by or steps into our life is meant to stay, just as some answers are only for that moment in time.

Those who stick around become fellow pilgrims on the journey. Welcome fellow Pilgrims—Seekers of Your Destiny. This is where Synchrodivinity comes in—Do you believe it was by accident or coincidence that you picked up this book? Was it a coincidence that you are exposed to this Reasoning? Synchrodivinity is a word used to describe the events that happen to assist us on our spiritual path. As a Life Coach I help people connect with their life's purpose. Synchrodivinity is a Life Coach of the highest level, assisting you on your path. It coaches us through people, events, dreams, patterns, animals, nature, numbers, the planets and spirit guides. Synchrodivinity is ever present in every happening in your life but we are often not paying attention so patterns repeat, things get bigger, so as to get our attention. If we are not willing or have closed our eyes on our path we will not see the signs directing us. *The Alchemist* by Paulo Coelho is all about this path to find what he calls "Our Personal Legend."

> "For the willing, destiny guides them
> For the unwilling, destiny drags them"   Seneca

I would rather be guided on my path than drug through this life. How about you?

When we have those times in life when we feel like life is dragging us along, it is a good time to take a look to see if it is a result of not allowing ourselves to be guided? Maybe we do not have our eyes open to the signs. There is Synchrodivinity and there is what Deepak Chopra calls Synchro Destiny. He says Synchro Destiny is the mysterious ingredient from the unconscious that all great leaders harness. He describes it as a coincident that contains a purpose, meaning or intention. Similar to Jung's Synchronicity, Syncho Destiny is about Intention and Manifesting what you are here to do.

Synchrodivinity is the Infinite Guide that comes by way of signs, omens, intuition, events, people and timing.

Synchrodivinity is the sign posts; it is the Infinite Life Coach to help you fulfill your Destiny. Synchrodivinity assists and supports your

Sacred Contract, your Highest Purpose and Intention for Being. Synchrodivinity is your conscious awareness that all that is happening is to guide you to your Destiny.

Synchro Destiny is the manifesting of your destiny through conscious awareness and deliberate Intent. Synchro Destiny is about Intention and Manifesting.

The most important question is: Do you believe you have a Destiny? Most major wisdom traditions teach us that we do.

Quran—There is not one of us but has his appointed position and we are verily ranged in ranks for service.

Talmud—All appointments are from heaven, even that of a janitor.

Christian—For I have great plans for you.

Jesus—Shall I not drink from the cup you have prepared for me?

Confucianism—Though nothing happens that is not due to destiny, one accepts willingly only what is one's Destiny. That is why he who understands destiny does not stand under a wall on the verge of collapse. He who dies after doing his best is following the way, dies according to his proper Destiny. It is never anyone's Destiny to die in fetters.

So what is your Destiny? It is not to be in fetters—in other words to be imprisoned, not allowing the freedom to be who you were created to be. We were created to be the outward expression of the inward Divinity.

One way to know your Destiny is to know what brings you joy. Another is to ask yourself—How do you wish to be known? Is there a word or a phrase that you would want to be described as or spoken of? If so, what would it be? In my workshop, Fulfilling Your Destiny, I ask "What do you want to be known for?" I ask people to write their eulogy to help them find their purpose for being here on earth. I reinforce this principle by having participants create a Vision Board that can assist in manifesting their destiny.

For this moment, close your eyes and go within and ask this question, "What do I want to be known as?" Is it loving? Is it generous? Is it wise? Whatever it is, that is part of your Purpose. It is part of your Destiny. Paulo Coelho, author of The Alchemist, a book I highly recommend, said "When a person really desires something all the universe conspires to help the person realize his dreams." Synchrodivinity is the universe conspiring to help us realize our <u>dreams</u>.

We must set an Intention, for you see Intention is a force like gravity. Intention creates energy, energy CREATES and MANIFESTS. The universe supports the process.

Synchrodivinity assists us with our intentions but this means we must first know our intentions. Once we know, we must look for the signs that will tell us which direction to go, what is next, where to stop and where to find the needed guidance. Remember this information comes from signs, dreams, animals, nature, people and/or events.

Here are some tools for seeing and understanding the Synchrodivinity in your life or ways to align your spiritual ducks:

1. Slow down. Meditate—Ask your higher self, the spirit within to reveal direction and wisdom. It is all within.
2. Connect with nature, animals and spiritual seekers

3. Keep a journal of events that happen and dreams that have similar patterns. Log these events metaphorically and metaphysically. Share with other seekers.
4. When you do receive signs, TAKE ACTION! Don't just say, oh that is interesting, what a coincidence.
5. Remind yourself frequently what it is you want people to see in you, know about you, for that is part of Your Destiny.

I now close this Reasoning with a slightly modified reading from *Warrior of Light* by Paulo Coelho; it is a companion book to *The Alchemist*. *The Alchemist* is all about living your Destiny, Your Personal Legend—It is about doing so by paying attention to Synchrodivinity.

"The moment that we begin to walk along it, the Warrior of the Light recognizes the Path.

Each stone, each bend cries welcome to you. You identify with the mountains and the streams, you see something of your own soul in the plants and the animals and the birds of the field.

Then, accepting the help of God and of God's Signs, you allow your Personal Legend to guide you toward the tasks that life has reserved for you.

On some nights, it seems you have nowhere to rest, on others, you suffer from insomnia. "That's just how it is," thinks the Warrior: "I was the one who chose to walk this path. My Path is my destiny. I create it and the universe supports it." In these words lie all your power: You chose the path along which you are walking and so have no complaints.

Reasons to Go Within—Personal Application

Coaching Questions:

1. How do you understand the difference between Synchrodivinity and Synchro Destiny?
2. Do you believe you have a sacred contract with the Infinite?
3. Do you know your sacred contract? If so, what is it?
4. Do you believe everything that happens is part of a bigger purpose than the present moment?
5. What is it you want to be remembered for? This is your Synchro Destiny.

Guided Mediation

Oh the joy that is this moment—aligning and attuning to the One. We find our home in breathing. Aligned with the One who prepares this moment with tranquility and fountains of livingness, joyfully knitting ourselves together from within. Affirm that all you do is guided by a loving energy that is present to assist you to live your Destiny, your highest good, to direct you to your ultimate joy. Affirm that you welcome all signs and messages from Spirit. Affirm you are a Child of the Cosmos and birthed from the Most Infinite. What is it you may need to know regarding your path? Ask for signs to guide you—ask for Synchrodivinity moments. Affirm you will be conscious of the Synchrodivinity in your life.

Section IV

Energy

Energy Introduction

One can hardly live and not hear about this thing called ENERGY. Actually we cannot live without ENERGY. Everything is made up of ENERGY.

In these next four Reasonings we will look at some of the strongest fields of energy. Love is the highest form of energy because there is no greater love than the Divine Love. It is the energy of the Spirit. We are the conduits that channel divine energy from the Divine Source. It is important for us to understand the principles of energy and the power of our own energy if we are to make a difference in our lives and the lives of others.

Love Is the Energy of the Soul

When love is blocked, it is still never stopped, because God is the Source and that supply never ends, but when blocked it is blocked by FEAR! Do you agree? Everything is Love or Fear—Please refer to *A Course in Miracles* if you would like more information on this topic.

We are all connected to the Source of Unconditional Love, God! Love flows through us but if we have a kink or a leak in the conduit, call it fear, we will suffer individually and the whole world suffers because we feel cut off from the supply. The cut off valve is fear. But the supply source is always present.

In *Mastery of Love*, Don Miquel Ruiz says, "What you are is a force, a force that makes it possible for your body to live, a force that makes it possible for your whole mind to dream magnificent dreams." When fear is cut off from the source of unconditional love in our soul, energetic patterns change. You are Life itself. God is life, God is love, God is energy. We are life, we are love and we are energy. Love is the highest expression of that energy. It has the most power and sends the highest vibrational frequency. We feel it vibrationally in our hearts. When we are feeling loving, demonstrating love, we feel the ENERGY of the soul. The soul is where the inner world meets the outer world!

When we are being loved, we feel it vibrationally. Words do not even need to be spoken. We see it in the eyes of the one giving love. A good example of this is when your pet looks at you adoringly with those most trusting eyes. My daughter has a plaque in her home that says "I want to be the person my dog thinks I am." I want to be the person God thinks I am.

We see it in another's eyes when we forgive or ask for forgiveness. We see love. Everything that does not look like love, feel like love, is FEAR. When we are in fear we are disconnected from love.

We are told by the sages of the ages that God is Love. Psalms 100:5 "For the Lord is good and his love endures forever, his faithfulness continues through all generations."

It does not matter what your mother did, your father did or what either of them did not do. It does not matter what your significant other, friend, sister, brother did or did not do. Love surpasses generations and people's situations. God's love does not see anything but LOVE!

Remember, fear is: "False Evidence Appearing Real." N.D Walsch

Joseph Campbell said "The cave you fear to enter holds the treasure you seek." For me, that means the light in the darkest place is love. Human relationships are not easy especially with the ones we are most deeply connected to.

Vincent Van Gogh knew this when he cut off his ear for love. He said "Love always brings difficulties, that is true, but the good side of it is that love gives us energy."

Sri Sthya Sai Baba explained the concept of Divine Love this way: "It is only when you have the grace of knowing Divine Love can one endeavor deeply into human love, just like you can only enjoy the breeze of a fan when you have both the fan and the electrical energy to operate it."

Think of yourself as a fan and God as the energy source that operates it. Now think of Love as the switch that turns it on. Remember the

Source of power is always present but we control the switch—just as we turn on the faucet of the hose that waters our garden of life. Love is the energy of your soul! Nourish your soul and your life with love for yourself and for others.

Reasons to Go Within—Personal Application

Coaching Questions:

1. When love is blocked, it is still present. Do you believe that? Please explain your reasoning.
2. What part does fear play in blocking the energy of love?
3. What does Joseph Campbell's quote "The cave you fear to enter in holds the treasure you seek," mean to you?
4. How does the above quote apply to love?
5. Do you believe one can love another more fully if they know Divine Love? What is the reason for your belief around this thought?

Meditation:

Get comfortable, relax, breathe with the intention of just relaxing. If you will, feel your body just melt into your chair. Send your breath to your heart, the energy seat of love, the forth chakra. Place your hand on your chest and feel your heart beat, sending life to your body. Imagine each beat as a vibration of energy, the color coming from your heart vibrates pink: it is the love color. Now send your breath to the energy field around your body, it also is vibrating love. Love from with, love from without. Only love! You are surrounded by love within, without. There is no end to the love vibrating from within and from without you. Whenever you become filled with fear, call on this awareness. Know there is an endless supply of love coming from the Source of All Love. Next time you think anything but love, release it to love. Next time you start to speak of anything that may not be kind, release it to love. Draw on the energy of the soul to support you, that energy is pure love, infinite, divine love. Remember the soul is where the inner world meets the outer world and the energy of infinite love brings them into unison.

And so it is!

The Energy of Health and Vitality

We are usually more familiar and comfortable with term "energy" when we speak of our physical vitality. We say things such as "I am low on energy" or "I am running out of energy" to describe how we feel physically. Speaking and thinking of energy from our physical bodies seems to makes sense.

Many of us do know that everything is energy. Our body is energy in solid form, congealed energy. Remember that our thoughts matter because thoughts create matter. Everything that ever was, first was a thought. We were a thought in the Creator's mind, if you will. The thought was then created into physical matter.

Our body is temporal. It is made up of cells, atoms, vibrations and electrical responses. Some even believe that the only reason we have a body is to hold our Spirit while on this earth; we must have a congealed form to hold the energy of our Spirit. Biblical thought says, "What know you not that your body is the temple of God?" N. Douglas Walsh author of the series of *Conversations with God* books suggests there could be another thought to the idea of our body and our soul. I quote "The soul is the energy of life that exists within and around (the aura we have is the vibration of the energy radiating from within.) The Soul of God holds in the Universe, the soul of humans hold in each individual body."

With the new research equipment that collects data, scientists can now measure energy fields around the body as well as in the body. Let's think about this for a moment, what if the body is not the container for the Soul, but the other way around, the soul is the container for the body? The body could not exist without the soul. When we die our soul leaves and our spirit leaves. It does not die.

What if we die because our soul/spirit no longer needs our body or our body is not representing our spirit well? Think about it, what if?

It is a pretty interesting thought, God being the container for the universe—The universe is not the container for God—then why couldn't our body and soul work the same way? The universe is not the container for God—God is the holder of the Universe. So what if the body is not the container for the soul, the soul is the container for the body! I am not sure of the validity of this theory but I think it does deserve some pondering. If this is true, disease and death could be the Spirit's way of saying the body cannot support or match the energy of our soul. When considering the Energy of Health and Vitality it is important to consider how we look at our body, our beliefs about our body and the Energy that affects our well-being physically and spiritually. Our soul may make the decision to leave based on how our body is holding up and honoring our Spirit. Bev, a member of Spirit Space after hearing this Reasoning, shared with me that this Reasoning forever changed how she looked at her body.

Dr. Bruce Lipton in his ground breaking research in the field of new biology suggests and has supporting research that radically changes our understanding of life, our health and our Spirituality. His work shows that genes and DNA do not control our biology, that instead DNA is controlled by signals from outside our cells, including the energetic messages emanating from our positive and negative thoughts. In other words our health, our vitality, our actual physical make up can be changed by our thinking, our thoughts. I strongly recommend you read *The Biology of Belief* by Dr. Bruce Lipton. I quote: "It is my sincerest hope that you will recognize that many of the beliefs that propel your life are false and self-limiting and that you will be inspired to change those beliefs. You can take back control of your life and set out on the road to health and happiness."

Whether you believe that the body is the container for the soul or the soul is the container for the body—Your body is very important to your Spirituality and Health.

What is known by science and sacred writings is: What you think will determine and affect your physical health and energy. From the Bible, "What so ever a man thinketh, so is he." And from the words of Buddha, the Dhammapada, "The mind is the forerunner of all actions. All deeds are led by the mind, created by the mind. If one speaks or acts with a corrupt mind, suffering follows. If one speaks or acts with a serene mind, happiness follows. As surely as ones shadow."

<u>Every thought that betrays your highest, most holy self is a betrayal that leads to both, mental and physical suffering and unhappiness</u>!

I could not speak of thoughts, health and vitality without speaking of Louise Hay's work for over 40 years; author of *Heal Your Body, Heal Your Life*. She is living proof that physical symptoms can be reversed by changing your thoughts. Please read her story, read her books. She reminds us that the point of power is right here and right now in our own minds through the energy of thought. For every physical suffering, there is a mental thought pattern that as Buddha said is corrupt, meaning <u>not true</u> to your most holy self. Or in other words, it is not matching the energy and spirit of the Source of all things. Your highest, most holy self is who you really are! This causes a conflict in your body. There are many ways to a healthy body. There are many modalities. All can work or none will work if you are not applying the energy of healthy thoughts. Consider the placebo effect—your thoughts make it work!!

I just finished a book by Dr. C. Norman Shealy, founding president of the American Holistic Medical Association, *Energy of Medicine*, which I also recommend. This book helps with the understanding of medicine, spiritual connection and energy.

Years ago many read *The Anatomy of an Illness* by Norman Cousins. He wrote about his journey to healing using laughter and holistic medicine in conjunction with recommendations from his medical doctor (now it is called integrative medicine). In the 1970s there was not a word for it. I had not yet reached my path into New Thought and had never heard of the Fillmores but I was fascinated by this idea. This man proved your mind can cure your body.

Here I am 40 years after it was written, still intrigued. Charles and Mrytle Fillmore were cofounders of a movement known as Practical Christianity. They discovered the connection between physical health and spirituality. Mrytle believed that forgiveness along with affirmations could heal and extend your life and energy, as did Charles. Both were healed of maladies and lived long healthy lives.

This is what Myrtle said about energy and life, "When one turns to God, the Universal Source of supply, it is as though a button is touched and the light comes on. One makes a connection that unifies him with the Central Power plant within, The Kingdom of God, wherein one contacts all that is in God, the Substance and Life and Wisdom and Love, All of GOOD!" Mrytle said "Life is simply a form of energy and has to be guided and directed in one's body by one's intelligence."

I suggest you take a 3"x5" card or a piece a paper and write an affirmation now about your health. Please begin the affirmation with "I am . . . .". Begin with declaring that you are strong, healthy, free, wise, powerful, beautiful, successful and a child of God.

Meditation

In your mind say the words of your affirmation silently. Repeat that affirmation multiple times. See it in your minds eyes. Now feel it in your heart, see it, feel it!! Remember thought matters because it creates matter. My body is a sacred container for my spirit. My spirit is a sacred container for my body, they become ONE! I love my body. I love my Spirit! I love life, life loves me! I love Spirit and Spirit loves me.

Reasons to Go Within—Personal Application

Coaching Questions:

1. What do you believe about the body and the soul? Do you believe the body holds the soul/spirit or do you believe that the spirit holds the body?
2. Do you agree that your beliefs can determine your physical health?
3. How do you think forgiveness or unforgiveness affects the body? What role does it play in health?

The Energy of Money

In this day and age we use this term ENERGY so often to describe many different things. We say, "I have so little energy," meaning we are tired, or "I just ran out of energy." We sometimes say, "Oh she has such good energy," maybe this means you are feeling connected to her. Or how about, "He just saps the energy right out of me," maybe this means that he makes you tired or he frustrates you. Then there is "This room has negative energy in it." Maybe this means something bad has gone on here or you think it will. Then of course we talk about the Energy of Spirit. Spirit just energized me. I felt Spirit's energy. What is this thing we call—ENERGY?

Many of us heard Oprah on her last ABC network show (which I call her Reasoning) say "People, EVERTHING IS ENERGY. And ENERGY IS GOD." So call it Jesus, call it source, call it creator or call it universe. It is all energy and all God.

When I say ENERGY, I am talking about the Source, who I also call God. You can call it whatever you wish knowing that it is the Source of all that is!! Know that when I speak of energy, I am speaking of God, the universal source of all that is!

My Master Coach, Maria Nemeth wrote a book titled, *The Energy of Money*. Taking her workshop and reading her book opened my eyes about the energy of money.

Joseph Campbell called money congealed energy. The word congealed means pulled together to make solid form. Energy is made of moving atoms and molecules pulled together to create a solid form. Albert Einstein taught that there is one energy field that creates all matter. This energy field is the sole governing agency of all matter. The mind is the sole governing source of the body. Therefore the mind creates. What we think does matter for it creates matter.

What we believe and think about money has much to do with our abundance or lack of it. We are co-creators with the source of all. Our thoughts bring forth the creative energy that can create something into form. Dr. Bruce Lipton, author of *The Biology of Belief* tells us that energy is made up of moving molecules when brought to physical reality. Money therefore is moving molecules that congeal to become matter. Thoughts can create abundance or lack thereof. Money itself has no intrinsic value other than what our thoughts make of it. It is very important to understand ones beliefs and intentions concerning this energy. Depending on your background, you may have come to believe money is bad. Most all of us have heard the quotes from the Bible that seem to agree with this principle. Money is the root of all evil. Or how about the quote: "The Love of Money is the root of all evil," I Timothy 6:10. Or how about, "It is harder for a rich man to enter heaven than it is for a camel to get through the eye of a needle." Matthew 19:24. In Jerusalem there is a rock formation that creates a passage where a camel must get down on its knees to get though. Both of these verses are speaking of one's intention, not money itself. If you love money more than the source it comes from or you are not willing to humble yourself, money will be a source of harm and it will be difficult to connect to the Source. Money itself has no spiritual meaning. There are religious teachings that believe to have little is a sign of piety and service to God. There are those who shun wealth and even take vows of poverty. And there are those who believe having wealth is a sign, to have much means you have found great favor with God. Some say poverty and a humble life is a sign of an evolved soul, while there are others that say wealth and abundance is a sign of a highly evolved person who has mastered the art of manifesting. Abundance or lack is about your beliefs about yourself, your source, and energy, and not so much about God's beliefs about you. Thoughts become things. Molecules/atoms only become things through the process of creation. Creation happens when we receive an idea and set the intention to bring it into conscious reality. The Source of all—Divine Mind—God— Ultimate Energy will support us to bring it into physical reality.

Remember, it is not about Deserving.

We are the conduits to channel this divine energy that comes from the Source who does not say some are more deserving. For a moment think of yourself as a garden hose. The hose is connected to the source (water in this case), the water runs freely through us as long as the control is turned on. So we have the water turned on, this is done by our conscious connection to the Source (we do this through affirmations, prayer, intentions, service, through positive thoughts and gratitude).

As the water (energy) flows through the hose, it waters the gardens of our dreams, our lives but let's say for a moment, the hose springs a leak—we can leak by being unforgiving or we can get a leak from forgetting to be grateful. Another way of leaking energy is to not give back from all that has been given to you. These things cause leaks in our flow of abundance. The next thing you know, there is not much flowing out of the hose. The garden does not thrive because it is lacking the energy of water. Know that the source is always available, always on, as is the supply, but by our thoughts, actions and deeds we can get cut off from the abundant supply moving through us from the ultimate Energy Source. I must stop again and thank Maria Nemeth for being so enlightened and generous in her willingness to share her wisdom.

Now, let's go back to the idea of the energy of money. Everyone has a Prosperity Profile that was created around the belief of abundance.

If everything is created in mind through energy waves, it is important to take a good, long look at what you believe about money.

When I was a child, my uncle used to say, "Sherry baby, money just burns a hole in your pocket." We all know what he means with this comment. If I had it, I spent it! And it was true. We had an open account at our little grocery store, so I could go in anytime and get something and Mrs. Jones just charged it to my family's account. Then every two weeks when my uncle got his paycheck, they would pay the balance on the account. My family knew I would NOT misuse my privileges EXCEPT for when it came to friends. Then I would often take them into the store and let them pick out candy. I would say "Put it on the bill!" That generosity put my credit account to an end at age eight.

From this history, maybe you can understand my Prosperity Profile—I only knew generosity. My family was generous and trusting, so I think that way. I was encouraged to always share. We did not have much money. My uncle worked three jobs to help maintain our lower middle class life style. But what I did learn was that there is always enough and if you have something, share it. That has become my Energetic Prosperity Profile. Many have commented that I am a Manifestor. Meaning I create—The principles of Prosperity is what makes one have a High Energy Prosperity Profile. No matter what your Energy Prosperity Profile has looked like, no matter what your history has been, you can change it by changing your thoughts about Prosperity and Money.

Remember the following Principles of Prosperity:

1. It is Already Prepared—A reminder to us that the Source is always turned on
2. All Sufficiency—says the supply never runs out. I don't care what the economy says.

3. Giving and Receiving—For me this is my mainstay. I know the more I give the better off I am. I do not often speak about tithing—tithing is donating 10% of what you make, but I know it works. Anyone I have ever challenged to try it for 90 days also knows that this principle works. It is not just about the dollars, it is about the attitude, the mindset.
4. Not Forgiving is the biggest leaker of the energy of money/ prosperity. I cannot emphasize enough that even if you give generously, if you have unforgiveness, there is a large hole in your conduit.
5. Ask for whatever you want to also supply and apply to all others.
6. Right Thinking—Positive intentions create positive results.
7. Gratitude—Remember to say thank you.

Reasons to Go Within—Personal Application

Coaching Questions:

1. List some of your beliefs about money.
2. What do you notice about these beliefs? Do they reflect scarcity or abundance? What about faith or fear?
3. What would you say is your Prosperity Profile? (This comes from your family of origin, your past personal choices and/ or your belief systems.)

Meditation

Breathe, Relax, Let Go and Release any concerns of lack of energy. Imagine a beautiful gold cord coming down from heaven and connecting at the top of your head. This cord is hollow; it is a conduit for all the energy from the source of <u>all</u> energy. It is always flowing. There is always a supply. There is a supply of all goods running through you like a river of life. It flows with abundance, whether it is material need, health and vitality or love. The supply is never ending. You repeat these thoughts and affirmations that keep the golden cord strong.

Principles That Can Change Energy Fields

Do you believe that you can walk into a room and change the energy in that space? Have you ever experienced someone else coming into a place or situation and within moments the whole scene seems different? This scenario is a demonstration of our ability to shift energy fields.

I have spoken often about the concept that we <u>do</u> affect the spaces we occupy, as Dr. Jill Bolte Taylor, author of *My Stroke of Insight* said, "Please be responsible for the energy you bring into this space."

After suffering a massive stroke that shut down her left brain, Dr. Jill Bolte Taylor, this left-brained, brain scientist had to rely totally on her right brain. Just as a reminder of brain function: the left brain is the rational, logical and verbal part of the brain. The right brain is the intuitive, creative, spiritual side. We need both to operate in this world the way we do. Most of us naturally lean more toward one side of the brain or the other.

I want to reason a bit further about something that Dr. Taylor said, "I have come to realize that the stroke was the best thing that could have happened to me because it taught me this euphoric feeling called peace—nirvana is never more than a mere thought away."

That is a very powerful statement, isn't it? Religious gurus and sages have been saying it for eternity, but when a brain scientist validates it, that is a whole new realm of understanding. I have thought about this statement often, "Peace—Nirvana is never more than a mere thought away." If that is so, then of course fear—chaos is also a mere thought away.

I teach a workshop called Eliminating Emotional Suffering. I created this workshop at a time when I was closer to the thoughts of fear than I was to peace. I count on the principles to shift my fear into peace or my hell into heaven—Nirvana. (You can find the principles to eliminate emotional suffering listed in the "Is Suffering Really Necessary" Reasoning.)

Let us go back to my beginning question: Do you believe you can change the energy of a space, a situation or a relationship by changing your thoughts? Thoughts create actions. Every action comes first in the form of a thought. Change your thoughts—Change your life.

Scientists have discovered that every thought represents an electrical charge of energy. Thought is energy. Energy fields are represented in people, places and things. They are spiritual, physical, personal, relational and/or financial and they are fields for energy to move. What we do with that energy is OUR RESPONSIBILITY!

We create the thoughts that lead to suffering; we also create the thoughts that lead to peace. I want to address three principles and if we are willing to practice these principles I believe it will change the vibrations or frequency of any situation.

First, let's do a short review on energy. Everything is made up of atoms. Atoms traveling at the speed of light become light. This happens by a vibrational frequency. God is light. God is energy. Spirit is energy. Our thoughts are energy because everything is energy (atoms). There are low level energy fields which are slower moving (less light filled) and when these fields are vibrating very slowly, negative frequencies are detected. High energy fields vibrate at a much faster frequency. Spiritually, positive energy fields travel at the speed of enlightenment, just as atoms traveling at the speed of light become light.

We are more than just our physical bodies. We are energy traveling either at the speed of enlightenment or we are energy separating at a low level of consciousness. One produces light—the other has little light power, it is not so energy efficient.

Think of our chakras—our lower chakras spin at a lower vibration and are connected to our sexuality, our survival, creativity and our human journey. Our upper chakras spin faster and are more connected to our spiritual journey.

The three principles that can shift the energy of any situation for each of us are:

1. The Principle of Separate Realities: What this means is "We do not see things as they are, we see them as we are," Anais Nin. Because we each see things from our own experiences and interpretation we each have a different thought system. We all filter things differently. Discord and judgment often happens because we believe the other person should see things our way. This is where judging begins. We judge our rightness and someone else's wrongness. Wars are fought because of this, broken relationships happen because of this. In my seven principles to eliminating emotional suffering (listed in the "Is Suffering Really Necessary" Reasoning), one of the seven principles is to avoid judgment and another is to give up the need to be right. Being "right" is most often a personal perspective. Facts can make up a physical reality, but when has proving yourself right and someone else wrong given you a feeling of Nirvana, Heaven or Peace? It usually just lowers the energy field to a level where the other person has to find a way to make you wrong. When we let go of judgment, we can better discern what is best for a situation. We can change the energy of a situation or

relationship by understanding and accepting that we all live in separate realities. We will be less likely to judge and there will be room for more compassion and acceptance. When we bring this kind of thought pattern to a space, negative energy has to shift to a higher vibration.

2. The Principle of Oneness: I have just spent some time suggesting that we all do not see things the same and the mere thought that we should, can cause problems. Now, the paradox is that we are all one! There is no exclusiveness in the mind of God. We can all see the highest potential when we see things from our divine eyes. When we make it about us, it becomes about our perspective and in this state we can get very dogmatic. When we see things from Divine Eyes, there is no separateness. There are no separate realities with God. When we accept that we are all one then we are more open. I Corinthians 12:12-21 is a most profound way to describe the beauty of separateness and oneness. "For just as the body is one and has many members, and all the members of the body, though many, are one body, so it is with Christ. For in the one Spirit we were all baptized into one body—Jews or Greeks, slaves or free—and we were all made to drink of one Spirit. Indeed, the body does not consist of one member but of many. If the foot were to say, 'Because I am not a hand, I do not belong to the body,' that would not make it any less a part of the body. And if the ear were to say, 'Because I am not an eye, I do not belong to the body,' that would not make it any less a part of the body. If the whole body were an eye, where would the hearing be? If the whole body were hearing, where would the sense of smell be? But as it is, God arranged the members in the body, each one of them, as he chose. If all were a single member, where would the body be? As it is, there are many members, yet one body. The eye cannot say to the hand, 'I have no need

of you,' nor again the head to the feet, 'I have no need of you.'" Each country in the world has different beliefs, yet the people inhabiting the country are part of the whole human race. They are different yet the same. As Jim Rosemergy, a Unity minister puts it, "Our God is Love. Our Race is Human and Our Religion is oneness." Together we are one humanity and divinity. It is our differentness that creates individuality. It is our sameness that creates connection.

3. The Principle of Priorities: This principle can shift the energy field by keeping everything in perspective. In any given situation, whether it is perceived as good or negative energy, the energy can be shifted by knowing what is important to you. Knowing what your intention is in any situation will give you clarity to proceed with that energy. If what I want is for you to understand my perception (not necessarily agree with it) and that becomes my priority then I would need to be clear that I want understanding. If this is the case then my actions would support that priority. If my intention is to make you wrong so that I can be right, then my actions will support that too. If my priority is to demonstrate Divine Love, my actions would be in accordance and consequently congruent with that intention. Knowing one's Priority or Intention can shift energy. That is why I enjoy life coaching so much. I get to help others live their highest intentions by shifting energy fields. Peace, Creativity, Joy, Laughter, Dreams and Goals are never more than a mere thought away.

I urge you to realize that we all have separate realities. We need to embrace our oneness with every creation on this planet because we were all created by the same manufacturer. We can still honor our individuality. This is our foundation and with this we can more clearly establish our priorities based on what is important and that will shift the energy of any space. Remember that the most important space is the space between our ears!

It is worth remembering that a very long time ago, before any of this talk of energy was part of the knowledge base, wisdom spoke through a humble priest, St. Francis. The Peace Prayer as I call it shows us how to change the energy of any space.

> "Lord, make me an instrument of your peace.
>
> Where there is hatred, let me sow love.
> Where there is injury, pardon.
> Where there is doubt, faith.
> Where there is despair, hope.
> Where there is darkness, light.
> Where there is sadness, joy.
> O Divine Master,
> grant that I may not so much seek to be consoled, as to console;
> to be understood, as to understand;
> to be loved, as to love.
> For it is in giving that we receive.
> It is in pardoning that we are pardoned,
> and it is in dying that we are born to Eternal Life."

Consider bringing the wisdom of St. Francis with you to any space. In doing so you will be able to answer my question positively: "Do you believe you can change the energy of any space with certainty?"

Reasons to Go Within—Personal Application

Coaching Questions:

1. Peace is only one thought away and so is fear. What practical application could you practice to increase peace and decrease fear?
2. Which of the three principles for shifting energy seemed to be the most difficult? What would it take on your part to shift that belief?
3. Do you believe you can shift the energy of a space? If so, what principles do you believe in that demonstrate this?

Section V

Suffering

Suffering Introduction

There is no question that in being on this planet, we have all experienced suffering. In the Buddhist tradition one of the principles is that suffering is the reality of life. In the Christian faith, the one most revered suffered terribly. The first Reasoning in this series of Reasoning asks if suffering is necessary. We do know that most of the world's suffering is self-created suffering. Stress, burnout, illness, depression and anger are all symptoms of suffering. We seem to unconsciously create a suffering scale so that we can measure and compare our level of suffering to that of others.

Physical suffering is different from emotional suffering which is different from soul suffering. The one unifying piece about suffering is our mind. What we think does create our destiny. Thoughts become things. Some thoughts lead us to joy, others lead us to pain. These Reasonings will lead you to Gandhi's words "Peace begins with me."

Is Suffering Really Necessary

A few years ago on a cold January day, I began a journey to personally find out the answer to <u>that</u> question. Some of you know this story and some of you will be hearing it for the first time. It isn't one I like to repeat but I love to speak of the wisdom that I was given because of it.

A call came from my son who lives in Costa Rica. He was to undergo a series of two eye surgeries to repair some very serious damage he experienced as a result of a diving accident a few months prior. I almost always know it is Clint calling before I pick up the phone. When the phone rang I thought it can't be Clint, he still has one more surgery, so he won't call until tomorrow. It was him. He said "Mom, I see better than I ever have" (he was legally blind as a child, but with the help of very strong prescription lenses, he could see normally.) The diving accident Clint experienced had the potential of taking his sight away.

Now let me take you back to the phone conversation. After Clint said, "I see perfectly. There will not be a need for the second operation," he said "Please get a pen and paper and write what I am about to say for I have no intention of repeating this or holding these words in my memory. The doctor said I will be completely blind within a few months. There is nothing the doctor can do but give me medicine to relieve the pain and pressure in my eyes and head."

I started suffering <u>immediately</u>! Like most suffering, it got in the way of the truth. It woke up with me in the morning, followed me through the day like a shadow. It then went to bed with me and haunted my sleep with night terrors of the worst kind. It soon became clear that I did not want to live this way. I would not be a victim! I refused to lose my faith so I did what I do; I sought for answers and spiritual wisdom. I started looking for truths that I could apply to get me through the day, the night, the next 24 hours. I would write them one by one on a black board that hung in my office. While I sat with my clients I could see it right above their heads.

One day my spiritual sister Johanna came by to comfort me and saw what had developed. It was seven statements, one for each day to help with my suffering. She said "This is not just meant for you. You MUST share it."

You have in your hands the result of my journey. Is emotional suffering really necessary? Emotional suffering hurts very badly. We do not have to suffer over and over again. Pain in this life is inevitable but suffering is optional. That was my mantra for many, many days. Deepak Chopra said "Suffering is pain held onto!" I am not denying the existence of the pain; I choose not to hold on to it. If and when I do hold on to pain, the suffering gets worse.

A Course in Miracles—"There are no problems, it is only in our mind." Rephrased, all the emotional suffering comes from our mind.

Science of Mind—"And so we suffer, not because suffering is imposed upon us, but because we are ignorant of our true nature."

The Four Agreements—"All human suffering is the result of believing in lies, mainly about ourselves."

Sufi—"Cause of all suffering is unreality, false belief systems operating as reality."

Buddha—Fourth Nobel Truth—"For suffering to end, mindfulness and conscious present living is required."

What seems to be echoed from many wisdoms is that emotional suffering is created by the following:

Mind—thoughts

Choices

Lack of willingness

We must practice our ability to live in a present conscious state of being.

How I got through the months that followed the news of Clint's condition was by incorporating these Seven Principles often. The seven principles were amazing for me because it helped me change my thoughts to the present moment, thoughts such as: he is not blind and he is alive. In this moment there was no need to suffer. I made choices that were based on true, not false belief systems of some future possibility. I focused on what was true NOW, for now is all that is real.

Carlos Costaneda said "We either make ourselves miserable or we make ourselves strong. The amount of work and energy is the same. But one gives us strength and the other creates fear."

Let's take a quick look at each of these principles to eliminate emotional suffering. Remember, this is an all day workshop.

1.   Respect and Value Yourself and all others. When we are valuing and respecting our self, we are not doing harm to

our self. Suffering hurts. It not only hurts us but others. Often when we are suffering we do not want to be alone, so we cause others to suffer so we can have company.

2. Give up the Need to be Right—This is the "do not be attached piece of suffering." We suffer so much just because we want to be right more than we choose peace. Wars are about needing to be right. Arguments with friends, families and between couples are often about the need to be right. Not forgiving is about the need to be right. The key word is NEED. We all feel good when we are right but when we NEED it to feel good, we are hooked. *The Four Agreements* state "If you are suffering in your life right now, it is a guarantee that this condition is tied up to some kind of attachment to the way you think things should be." Here are some truths about the need to be right:

   - There are some people that you will never get to be right with because of the law of Attraction. If you are a person that has to be right, you are going to only attract more of "I need to be right people," and when this happens, no one gets to be right.
   - Being right is not all it is cracked up to be. Ask yourself what is the price for being right? Often, the price is alienation and lack of PEACE. What is your PEACE worth to you? In the whole scheme of life, were your most memorable, loving, spirit-filled moments ever about being right?

3. Avoid Judgments. We seem to get hooked into judging ourselves and others. This causes great suffering. I have learned that the less I judge others, the less I have to forgive, the more at Peace I am. Ram Dass suggests this method for eliminating judgment from our lives, "When

you catch yourself grumbling about someone else, own it as a projection and say, 'And I am that too.'" Whoa, that puts judging in a whole new light! Suffering also comes from judging what is happening and not accepting that God has everything under control. There is a Divine Order.

4. Forgive Instantly. We all know how important forgiveness is. It is included in the healing and prosperity principles. This principle is a little more radical. Do it instantly. The longer we harbor unforgiveness, the more we will suffer. Forgive quickly even if you must process it later. If we remember that unforgiveness causes our own suffering, we have an incentive to forgive sooner rather than later, which means less suffering. The word forgive means to give up all claims, to punish, to release, set free, get over. This means we are set free, we do not experience the pangs of punishment to ourselves that unforgiveness brings.

5. Keep Your Word. You may wonder how keeping one's word eliminates suffering. How many times have you suffered because you did not keep your word? How many times have you suffered because you used unkind words against yourself or others? The Dalai Lama said "Every human being should realize that the future of humanity is dependent on their present actions, thinking and words." *The Four Agreements* states "All the magic you possess is based on your word. Depending on how it is used, it can set you free or enslave you."

6. Stop Being Offended—Psalms 119:165 "Great peace have they which love thy way: and nothing shall offend them." Being offended is a choice—if we make a choice to be offended we then must defend. One of the biggest assumptions of life is that others feel and think the way we do. When they do not, we often make it about us. It is not about us!! From *Conversations with God*, "When feeling

offended, go first to your Highest thought about yourself and imagine the you that you would be in this moment if you lived that thought." Buddha in the Dhammapada says "If a man has a hand free of wounds, he can take poison in his hand. The poison cannot penetrate the hand that is free of wounds."

7. Practice Gratitude—What more can anyone say. Saying thank you is the CROWN. Whenever I start to suffer, I choose an attitude of gratitude. I am in the presence of Grace. As Anne Frank said "There is always some beauty left in nature, sunshine, freedom, in yourself. Look at these things and you will find yourself again, and God. This will help you to regain your balance."

A post note, my son still has his eyesight five years later. We are grateful.

Reasons to Go Within—Personal Application

Coaching Questions:

1. After reading about my story that led me to suffering, what experiences came to mind in your own life that have caused you to suffer?
2. How did you stop your suffering?
3. Reading over the seven steps to Eliminate Emotional Suffering, which one/ones could have made a difference in past sufferings and how?

Chakra Meditation

You may want to record the following and play it when doing this mediation.

Breathe—find a comfortable space within yourself. This is the gift you are giving yourself in this moment. For you have no other moment in time but this moment. Nothing can be except what happens in this moment. In your body are many energy sources all giving you life, giving Chi, Prana, energy from these energy sources called chakras flows life. It starts at the top you head, closest to heaven and flows down through your spine, supporting and sustaining your Being.

For the next few moments we are going to honor each energy source and the ability it has to assist in eliminating emotional suffering. Take three deep breaths. Place your left hand on the lowest part of your stomach (hands from the naval). Let your right hand rest palms up receiving the divine love.

O the joy that is in this moment, aligning and attuning to the One. We find our home in breathing. When feeling deeply confused by life, we return to being untied inside by love. We soften all that is rigid within, our muscles, our hearts that have received blows. You feel the warm arms of compassion embracing you. You radiate from love. Aligned with the One who prepares the ground for all tranquility, we are fountains of Livingness joyfully knitting ourselves together from within. What is stealing your PEACE like a thief in the night? Are you willing to Release, Surrender and Extend Grace to yourself. And SO IT IS!

Chakra 1—Root—See a beautiful wheel of ruby red light circling in clockwise direction, similar to a ceiling fan running at a slow speed. Feel yourself opening up at the base of your spine. You notice how free you feel. You are free to love and respect yourself as you were created to do. You know in this moment you are the creation of all that is good, created by the creator of Good. You also know in this moment that this is truth for all of us. There is nothing you or anyone else can do that changes the perfection of our Creator. This is our roots, your heritage. Nothing else is deeper than this root. Right now remind yourself that you value and respect yourself and all others. Give thanks.

Chakra 2—Sacral—Move your left hand up a few inches, just below your naval. See a most beautiful wheel of orange light in the middle is a clean white circle. It is the same size as your Red Root Chakra. It is spinning just a wee bit faster. Feel yourself free from any need to prove anything to anyone. In this moment you know this truth. There is no need to perform, prove or win. There are no battles because you are not at war. You know only PEACE. You are free from the need to be Right. Right now remind yourself of that Truth. Give Thanks.

Chakra 3—Navel—Move your hand up and let it rest on your navel. See a most beautiful wheel of yellow light that looks like sunshine, yellow and white sparkling sunlight. This wheel spins slightly faster yet is the same size as the other lights. Feel all the energy of love compassion. You are in this moment. The best you, you can be. You accept this in yourself and others. Your words repeat I am the best me at this moment. And so is everyone else. Repeat "We all are capable of our highest and in each moment we can transform ourselves." Right now remind yourself that you are free of judging yourself, others, events. Give thanks.

Chakra 4—Heart—Move your hand and place it on your heart. See a most beautiful emerald green light. White bursts of light stream from it. This wheel spins rapidly. It radiates unconditional love for yourself and all living things. Peace radiates from your heart chakra.

It is the entrance to your soul. Your heart chakra speaks love, hears love and radiates love. Whisper these words as you breathe into your heart; I am love, I LOVE, WE ARE LOVE. Give thanks.

Chakra 5—Throat—Move your hand and gently place it on your throat. You see a sky blue wheel of light spinning at a fast speed. As this sky blue light surrounds your throat, your vocal cords, vibrations of the intention to speak. Kindness, truth and compassion to yourself and all others pulsate in your throat. You hear tenderness and love in your ears. You are free to keep your word to yourself and others.

Chakra 6—Eye—Move your hand up to the middle of your forehead, right between your eyes. You see an Indigo blue wheel of light. In the center is an oval shaped eye. The eye flashes with white purple, blue lights. This light fills you with wisdom of the ages. It is where any question has an answer. You are in your highest knowing here. This eye sees more than the human eye. It sees as God sees. It sees Love and Forgiveness on offenses. Only compassion for the journey is present. Give thanks.

Chakra 7—Crown—Place your hand on the top of your head. This is your crown of Glory. This wheel is royal purple radiating Love and Divine guidance and protection. Feel the noble, royal purple energy from the highest source moving over the top of your head down through your third eye, throat, heart, naval, stomach out through your feet grounding you in TRUTH. You are blessed and highly favored as a Divine Creation of ENERGY and LOVE. Give thanks!

Running From Our Shadow

Have you ever tried to run from a shadow? It is impossible because it just chases you, doesn't it? It is similar to the Greek mythology thought about dragons. The legend says that if you run from a dragon it will chase you. If your draw your sword and fight it, for each drop of blood that falls, another dragon will appear.

The shadow side is sometimes referred to as our dragon or our demons. Well, in Greek mythology the only way to tame a dragon is to face it and tell the truth. To understand our shadow or dark side is to face it and find the truth. The coaching term for this is Look, See—Tell the truth. For the truth does set us free!

I would like to share a glimpse into what we do not like to look at, and that is our shadow. It is not so popular in New Thought to even speak of it. It is much more pleasant to look toward the light. Yet, by not looking at our shadow we miss the reason for the light and we lose a tool of enlightenment. Dr. Carl Jung, the Swiss psychiatrist was the first to connect the phrase shadow as part of our psyche. He said:

"One does not become enlightened by imagining figures of light but by making the darkness conscious."

Leonard Cohen, the singer and song writer wrote "There is a crack in everything and that is how the light gets in." Another songwriter for this generation, Taylor Swift, wrote these words: "I guess you really did it this time, left yourself in your warpath. Lost the balance on a tightrope."

Joseph Campbell said: "We must learn to integrate light and dark. For when we stumble, there your treasure lies."

Just what does that mean? Well in coaching terms, everyone and everything is our coach/teacher. Some teachers come in light form and we love these teachers. Some come in hard or dark form—but both teach us. We must be willing to learn our life lessons no matter who the presenter is.

The experience of pursuing enlightenment can cast a long shadow. It is in the seeking of the light that one finds darkness, for that is when our dark side becomes more visible. In other words we are more conscious of it because we are in the light.

As with a literal shadow, one cannot see your shadow unless there is light. Literal shadows are made when an object stands in the path of light and blocks the light from shining, thereby creating darkness. I urge you to reread the previous sentence as there is an important message delivered in it.

Anything that blocks light can form a shadow. When light comes from directly above you will not see a shadow. But when it comes from offside or at an angle, a shadow is cast by the object that is preventing the light to filter through. Moving the light source closer to an object can make a shadow appear larger while moving the light source away can have the opposite effect.

Shadows happen when the light is blocked. Is that not how shadows work metaphysically? When we block our light (life light), darkness can appear within us. Being conscious of that allows us to shine light directly to it! When there is pure light from above (our highest), one will not experience darkness. But when we get out of balance or we are not fully conscious, the light is blocked from within casting a shadow on our Spirit. It becomes our teacher.

Dr. Carl Jung believed that we were born with a shadow side. He explained the shadow as being the person we would rather not be. It is the part of us that we reject and want to hide away like an unwanted, disturbed child, locked in the basement of our psyche, always aware that at any time someone could discover its existence. The shadow is the message we hear in our heads that says "I am not good enough" or "I am not worthy." Dr. Jung suggested we must sometimes go into the dark in order to cast light and make the darkness light. Some have defined the shadow as the opposite of good or the opposite of light. I do not believe it is the opposite. I believe it is the part of the balance of being. Buddhists and Taoists teach that it is quite necessary to seek the light within the darkness and recognize the darkness within the light. It is not static, it is moving, vibrating constantly balancing us: It is a reflection or a mirror. It reminds us of the light.

All things must exist in balance in order for anything to be its mirror. Shadows exist to mirror light. When we become resistant or afraid to look at the things in ourselves that we resist or detest, we create more shadows: fear, despair, sadness and anger. It is similar to running from the dragon. The dragon is always breathing hot fire down our necks. The more we resist, stabbing with our sword of denial, the more baby dragons appear. **For what we resist, persists!**

The Dutch author, Touber in *A Crash Course In Enlightenment* asks and answers the following question:

How do you get to know your own shadow so we may cast light on it?

Answer: By looking at what you are projecting onto others. What bothers you in others? What hurts you? What do you judge or reject? That is your shadow. Anis Nin said "We do not see things as they are, we see them as we are." That is our shadow and this is our light. Touber suggests the way to cast light on your shadow is through:

1. Meditative inquiry and consciousness
2. Asking questions such as: who am I in my highest? When I am showing up less than that, what is it I need to see and learn about myself?
3. Seeking and finding mentors. Be with people who truly stimulate you, challenge you and inspire you.

It is all about a willingness to look, see and tell the truth. It is honest consciousness.

Our journey is to accept ourselves all the way from the basement, a damp, dark, scary, hidden away place within, to the pinnacle, the attic where all our unclaimed valuables are stored. This is the crown chakra.

Walt Whitman speaking of this journey said: "I now realize I am larger, better than I thought. I did not know I held so much goodness." A shadow can only come if there is light. When was the last time you said after experiencing grief, guilt or fear, "My, how very enlightened and courageous I am to make this connection with a shadow for it means I am light?" Remember Dr. Jung said: "One does not become enlightened by imagining light but by making darkness conscious." A plant needs darkness to grow as much as sunlight. Twenty four hours of light would not allow a plant to become strong. The heat and light would parch it. When we come face to face with our shadows, let it not be said we are afraid of our own shadow. Let us look, see, and tell the truth. We learn our lessons in this process and raise our consciousness in order to live in balance with our light and our dark. To live in balance is to locate ground zero where we take no sides. We let them stand next to each other as they are.

Also, be open to the positive counterpart to the dark. It is the Best of the Least. This is alchemy, turning something less into something of more value. Uniting our light and our dark is what the fairy tale story of Beauty and the Beast symbolizes. There was beauty in the beast and vice versa. Their marriage is a symbol of the potential for happiness when light embraces our darkness and we don't repress the beauty in our being. When we are afraid of the shadow, we often repress it. We must see the Beauty in the Beast.

Reasons to Go Within—Personal Application

Coaching Questions:

1. Have you ever tried running from your shadow? If so, what was it about and how did running from your shadow work for you?
2. Dr. Jung believed "The shadow as being the person we would rather not be." He also thought we must sometimes go into the dark in order to cast light, to make the darkness light. What are your thoughts about this statement?
3. What is the best way to get to know your own shadow?
4. What would it take for you to be able to identify the shadows in your life?

Meditation:

Relax and Be—Knowing you are filled with light. You are the light of the world. Imagine you are in a beautiful garden, the sun is streaming through the trees. The only sound is that of the birds singing their melodious rhapsodies. You come upon a labyrinth, beautifully and delicately laid with colorful stones that reflect light. They are placed in a circle that goes into another circle and then another. You step onto the labyrinth and begin the meditative ritual of walking the circle of life which all others have gone before. Your mind is at peace yet also filled with an unexplainable anticipation. The closer you move toward the center of the circle, the brighter the light seems to become. You have now arrived at the center. Light pours into the circle and as you bask in the warmth and glow of the light, you see an object casting a shadow. You recognize you are the object that created the shadow. You want to run but instead you take a deep breath and realize it is a shadow, it is not you. You take another deep breath and decide to not run from it as you have so many times before but to face it breathing love and acceptance into your shadow. You become astutely aware that the fear is leaving you as does shame or guilt. A white light radiates from your heart and moves to the center of the shadow. You feel gratitude for this moment.

You hear yourself saying to your shadow "You are present because I am light. No shadow can happen without light. I acknowledge the light in me is the light in all things, including that which I fear and lack understanding." Remind yourself to not run away in fear when your shadow appears. Promise to shine more light into the moments of shadows. You suddenly realize that your shadow has blended into the light and all around you is a marriage of light and dark dancing like twilight. Both are showing off the miracle of creation with all the different hues. Give thanks and begin your labyrinth walk back to full light. And so it is!

Tears in a Bottle

Psalms 56:8 "Thou tellest my wanderings: put thou my tears into thy bottle: are they not in thy book?" Crying purifies and cleanses. It has been said in scientific experiments that there are 38 toxic chemicals in a tear of sadness and there is only one toxin in a tear of joy.

Isn't that a beautiful metaphor for love and compassion? The thought that God knows each and every distress we have. God knows every tear we shed. And they are so precious in God's sight that God would place them in sacred bottles. Years ago when this verse first came to my attention, I wondered what God was going to do with all those bottles. Then I thought, what do my bottles look like? In my mind I thought about how amazing and beautiful bottles can be. Mine are jewel toned and come in every shape and size.

When my son was very young, he started a long journey of honoring bottles. I would hear him upstairs in his room talking and I knew that no one else was there. I would climb the stairs and peek into his room only to find him speaking to his bottles. He had all his bottles that he had collected. Some were from the garbage cans, some from my vanity shelf and some from his little wanderings. He would be telling the bottles his thoughts about the world and about life. Here was my son at five or six years old, sharing his heart with those bottles. His love for bottles has never left him. He finds it very hard to throw away a bottle to this day. He finds beauty in the shape, the color and the substance that occupied the bottles. I have given much thought to this verse over the years, "Our tears are stored in bottles."

Tears represent sorrow and joy, don't they? We cry when there is pain and we often cry when there is joy. Tears are an expression of our humanness but also of our divinity. For tears represent compassion. There is nothing more divine than compassion. When I enfold myself in the magnitude of the metaphor that "God knows my wanderings, and puts my tears in thy bottle," this is what it means to me: My divine creator, source of all that is, knows our journeys into some very scary and sad places. They are but wanderings. Just as a small child can wander away from home, suddenly realizing they are feeling lost and far from their secure base, tears start to run down their little cheeks. They feel the loss of the comfort that comes from the source of all comfort, Father/Mother God. Then this wonderful God catches the child up into arms like a bottle gently catching tears, reminding us that we are loved and safe. ALL IS WELL!

Tears in a bottle also remind us of compassion. Compassion is often defined as Mercy, Kindness and Tenderness. Do you see your God as compassionate, a source of kindness and tenderness? If your Creator is not, then you have not met the Creator of your soul.

Revelations 21:4 "And God shall wipe away all tears from our eyes; and there shall be no more death, neither sorrow nor crying, neither shall there be any more pain for the former things are passed away."

II Kings 20:5 "I have heard your prayer, I have seen your tears, behold I will heal thee."

This is a description of heaven, the place that God resides. We know that Jesus said that the Kingdom of God, Heaven is within. It is within our self that all suffering stops. There is a place within us that has complete joy.

When on this physical, external plane, sorrow and fear come, but our God has so much compassion for us. Our tears are received with such Dignity as to be symbolically placed in bottles. Honoring our times of wandering and hurt, never judged but honored as my once small son honored his bottles and spoke to them with reverence and compassion.

When the word compassion comes up for me I cannot help but think of the Buddha of Compassion, Kuan Yin. She is known as the Divine Giver of Compassion. This is just one of many representations of Kuan Yin. After her enlightenment she took an oath to postpone her entrance into nirvana until she had helped every other sentient being to become enlightened. (Bodhisattva) Her oath ties her to humanity as Jesus the Christ tied himself to humanity.

Her name means the one who hears the cries of humanity. Originally Kuan Shin Yin was seen in male form and then the female Kuan Yin emerged. Now they are seen as one. Kuan Yin and The Christ have very similar archetypical symbolism. Both are seen as saviors. Both are represented by Compassion and for hearing the prayers and cries of the world.

The Easter story is often called the Passion story. Compassion is the meaning behind it all. The pain, sorrow and drama of life evolve into the transformation and the resurrection of life. Without compassion it is just a story without resurrection and transformation; it is a horror story.

With Compassion it is Transformation in the highest. It is our story.

Reasons to Go Within—Personal Application

Coaching Questions:

1. Do you see your God as compassionate or as a harsh authority figure?
2. How did you get that belief system? And does it work well for you now?
3. Kuan Yin is a beautiful image of compassion. Do you have an image of compassion that you can call on in times of sorrow? If so, please describe.
4. What is the purpose for tears?
5. If your tears could speak, what would they say?

Kuan Yin Meditation

The Kuan Yin Prayer for the Abuser submitted by Jonathan Granoff

- To those who withhold refuge, I cradle you in safety at the core of Being.
- To those that cause a child to cry out, I grant you the freedom to express your own agony.
- To those that inflict terror, I remind you that you shine with the purity of a thousand suns.
- To those who would confine, suppress, or deny, I offer the limitless expanse of the sky.

The full prayer is readily available on line. I have included a link below:

http://pierreterre.com/blog/kuan-yins-prayer-abuser

Burning or Burned Out

This is a most important question, are you Burning or Burned Out? We are either a burning torch or a burnt out match. As George Bernard Shaw put it, "This is true joy in life . . . Life is no brief candle, it is a sort of splendid torch which we get to hold on to for the moment and we want to make it burn as brightly as possible before handing it on to future generations." This is some of what our life is about. This is what gives us purpose. It is our contribution that creates the possibilities for our future and that of this planet. If the torch goes out, if the flame is extinguished and light goes out in the world, so goes the bright hope of the world, the hope to do one better than was done before.

Have you ever seen or been in a large group setting, maybe a prayer vigil where people are standing by each other with lit candles, in the darkness. All you see is flickering, dancing lights in what would be the dark abyss.

That is who we are in the world; we are light. But if our flame goes out, what is left is darkness, an empty abyss. There is a light from within that keeps our torch burning, that is our spiritual flame. There is also our actual physical energy source that keeps our external torch bright. Both are required to light up the world. I want to spend some time looking at these two energy sources.

Let's start with what was coined in the 1970s as Burn Out. We all have probably experienced this phenomenon on some level in our life. There are different degrees of Burn Out, just as there are different sizes of flames. The scientific definition of Burn Out sounds something like this: A condition that develops when one has been exposed to excessive or prolonged periods of stress creating exhaustion, diminished interest and problems related to managing life successfully. In the world of social research, the Maslach Burn Out Inventory measures Burn Out by asking a series of questions that determine mental/physical exhaustion, cynicism and inefficiency.

- Exhaustion is measured by one's energy level
- Cynicism is measured by one's negativity and pessimism and also one's level of ability to trust
- Inefficiency is measured by the level of focus, competency, quality of work/life

The research shows Burn Out can cause physical and mental health problems as well as social, relational and spiritual problems. Here are some of the symptoms and phases of Burn Out:

- A compulsive need to prove oneself
- Neglecting one's needs
- Compassion fatigue—a lack of empathy and compassion for others
- Depersonalization—living robotically
- Displacement of conflict—blaming others for your unhappiness
- Cynicism—A cynic is when you know the worth of everything but do not appreciate the true value
- Revision of one's values, what once was important no longer has meaning or seems of value
- Withdrawal, social and relational isolation
- Behavioral changes
- Inner emptiness—a lack of joy
- Overwhelmed much of the time
- Lack of energy

Many of these symptoms sound like a checklist for depression.

Personalities Most Likely to Suffer From Burn Out:

- Perfectionists
- Pessimists
- Type A People
- Those who need to be in control

Working Conditions that Contribute to Burn Out:

- Working too much, especially at something you are not committed to or truly believe in
- Working with people you do not get along with
- Jobs where productivity is emphasized more than quality
- Being expected to do too many things (wear too many hats)
- Work environments that do not include validation, appreciation or recognition
- Work environments that do not encourage the physical, mental, spiritual and relational well-being of its people
- Environments that do not create mentoring relationships
- Environments that do not support and encourage creativity and expression

I wonder how many people are being treated for depression when what is going on is Burn Out. A condition that develops when one has been exposed to excessive or prolonged periods of stress. I wonder how many people have lost their jobs or have been demoted because they were considered incompetent or too old and what they were was Burned Out. I wonder how many relationships have ended not just because of incompatibility or loss of love but ended because of Burn Out. Sure, I know there are people who are not competent to do the job required, and yes, of course people do get depressed. And relationships end because love ends. But I wonder if that is always the case.

If Burn Out happens as a result of stress, then something needs to be done about the stress level in the world. Heaven knows we probably live in one of the most stressful times in history. The stress is only exaggerated by our communication technology. Most of us have more than enough to be stressed out about in our own lives, then think about every piece of news, data, research, reports, photos and visuals of all the rest of the world's stress we encounter daily. Talk about information overload.

I believe we operate in a state of collected conscious and unconscious fears and stress. One of the definitions of stress is being pulled in two directions, the pull creates tension. Just as a guitar string being pulled too tightly can break, this stops the string/guitar from creating beautiful music. And just the right tension creates beautiful sound, so is stress.

There are stress hormones Cortisol and Norepinephrine that are released through our endocrine system. When this happens a number of physical symptoms can appear:

- The immune system slows
- Weight gain, particularly in the middle
- Increased blood pressure, heart rate
- Increased glucose (sugar in the blood)
- Decreased testosterone levels in males
- Irregular menstrual cycles, decreased desire to be physically intimate, reproductive issues, adrenal fatigue in women.

If we are to survive and thrive, we must reduce the stress in our lives. There are a couple of proven ways to address stress and to prevent Burn Out. Researchers say:

1. Learn to relax, finding joy in life

2. Reduce the number of demands and stressors
3. Connect with the Spiritual torch within

Stress is always going to be a part of life but I believe that Burn Out can be avoided most of the time. Here is how:

1. Be clear about your life purpose
2. Be objective in choosing what is really important
3. Cultivate the ability to say NO without guilt or fear. It does not serve you to cater to demands that do not align with your life purpose. Say yes to things and people that support your purpose/passion.
4. Do not procrastinate
5. If necessary renegotiate commitments when need be
6. Acknowledge your own humanity. You just cannot do and be everything

"Follow your bliss," Joseph Campbell.

De-stressors to try: meditation, hobbies, positive affirmations, time with good friends, exercise, humor, spiritual involvement, contributions. Choose to never be a prisoner of urgency. For some, everything will seem urgent.

Joan Borysenko, author of the book *FRIED, Why You Burn Out and How to Revive* says: "Burn Out is a disorder of hope and will suck the life out of competent, idealistic, hardworking people. Revival from Burn Out is always about the recovery of lost authenticity. It is waking up to who we are and realizing that heaven is not a destination but a state of mind."

Don Miguel Ruiz in *The Four Agreements* says: "The dream you are living is your creation. It is your perception of reality that can change at any time. You have the power to create hell and you have the power to create heaven. Why not dream a different dream? Why not use your mind, your imagination, and your emotions to dream heaven?"

We know we are responsible for our state of mind. We must be in tune to our inner wisdom for this wisdom will always lead us to JOY. Burn Out has been described as having no joy. Following our inner wisdom, or GPS, you must pay close exquisite attention to the cues, the Synchrodivinites and you must trust in your Purpose for Being, your dream.

You create the Dream, so Dream WELL!

Reasons to Go Within—Personal Application

Coaching Questions:

1. Read through the Maslach Burn Out Inventory and check off any that may pertain to you right now.
2. Read through the personality types that are more likely to suffer from Burn Out. Do any describe your personality?
3. Read through the working conditions that can contribute to Burn Out. Do you work in an environment that can be described this way?
4. Finally, go through the list of ways to reduce stress and Burn Out. What items could be helpful for you right now?

Meditation:

Become aware of your breath, how easily and naturally it serves you. Just breathe a few breaths. Notice the chair you are sitting in, how easily it supports you. Your breath and the chair you are setting on are all in alignment with their purpose. Remember the birds that enjoy the joys of spring, the squirrels who run and play and the waves that roll into shore and out again. Remember the sun that rises and sets without any worries. They are all are in alignment with purpose. Each is supported by the unusual energy. And so are you! Just breathe, give thanks and know you create your heaven and in heaven there is no Burn Out.

Section VI

Prosperity

Prosperity Introduction

The thought that prosperity comes from asking the right questions is a unique one. Yet, think about it, when you go to the doctor, to your financial consultant or to your boss to get what you want or need, you must know the questions to ask. Life is like the game of Jeopardy. It is in the question where you find the answer.

To understand and receive prosperity in any energetic form we must begin with the questions. This is where you will find your "Acres of Diamonds" and once you have this understanding, you will know what to do with your diamonds.

Asking and Receiving—Ask the Right Questions!

As a spiritual life coach, I am very aware of the importance of asking the right questions when assisting people in discovering their path. In my own life, part of my growth is to be able to receive. Isn't that interesting?

You must Ask to Receive—What a concept!

Two beloved quotes about Asking (questions) and Receiving (answers) come from two very different sources.

"Call on me and I will answer you, and will show you great and mighty things you don't know (you know)." Jeremiah 33:3 (Questions)

"Be patient toward all that is unresolved in your life and try to love the questions themselves." *Letters to a Young Poet*, Rainer Maria Rilke (Answers)

We must ask to receive and we must seek to find and through it all we must be patient.

William Shakespeare reminded us: "How poor are they who have not patience. What wound did ever heal but by degrees?"

Some time ago I pondered as so many have, what is important for me to know as I go deeper with God? All spiritual seekers (and we all are, some are just more aware of that wisdom than others) ponder this question. What is it I need to know to find my way in this life? What is my ontological purpose for being? As a result of that question, I came up with five questions to help me and others answer the Big Question. What is my Purpose? What gives my life meaning?

Francis Bacon said "A prudent question is one half the wisdom." Remember, the answer always is found in the question. It is like the game show Jeopardy.

Some important questions to ponder:

1. What is my purpose and how can I demonstrate it in physical and spiritual reality?
2. Do I have and/or do I think I have free will?
3. Who do I think God is?
4. Who do I think I am?
5. Who do I think everyone else is?

Think on these questions for yourself. This is the reasoning part of this Reasoning. I ask that we "Come Reason Together."

1. What is my purpose and how can I demonstrate it in physical and spiritual reality? In coaching, I try to ask questions that begin with What, How and When. I try not to begin with a Why as Why questions can cause the monkey mind to chatter. It is because if we ask why and we do not know the answer right away, we will get scared because we believe that we are all supposed to know it all right now. Isn't that what has been expected of us through much of our domestication? How many times can you remember adults saying "You should know better?" The interesting part of this situation is that adults then think they are the knowing, they do not believe that the child knows. We are always becoming—becoming is knowing. The knowing comes from within. Be still and know. It comes from curiosity. It comes

from asking questions. From Science of Mind, "We must realize that there is an intelligence within us that does know." It is within, not always from without. Go within first, and then figure out how to live it. That is the path for Reaching Out.

2. Do I have and/or do I think I have free will? What makes this question so important is the following: Do you believe you have a say so in your life? If you think you don't, all types of unhealthy things can happen: You can become a victim, a martyr. You can let others beliefs make decisions for you. You can become hopeless, cynical and powerless. Victor Frankl's work is so important in this area. Please refer to *Man's Search for Meaning* for more information. This question reminds us that we create karma, "You reap what you sow." I believe we are co-creators with the Infinite—Together we create. We are not puppets, having our strings pulled by the Great Puppeteer. We have choices!

3. Who do I think God is? Who is this Infinite that we are partners with? The answer to this question will affect how we do life. If we see God as judgmental, withholding, harsh, unforgiving we will live a life that will be just that. It will be difficult to ask and receive. If we see God as loving, compassionate, wanting us to have <u>all</u> abundance, then we will not be afraid to receive. We will live our life through the eyes of the Infinite and there will be infinite possibilities.

4. Who do I think I am? So, just <u>who</u> do you think you are? Have you ever heard someone say that to you? Or how about, who do you think you are, God's gift to the world? Well the answer is YES. We are God's gift to the world. I received a beautiful wooden sign for Christmas that says it this way: "What we are is God's gift to us. What we become is our gift to God."

5. Who do I think everyone else is? When we understand who we are, we then must look at who everyone else is. We don't get to be God's gift to the world when others are not. It does

not work that way. That is what we are acknowledging when we say Namaste—"I behold the God nature in you."

Asking questions is the only way to receive answers. Seek and you shall find. Ask and it will be given. I encourage you to ask prudent, seeking questions. Ask What and How questions to better understand the very important things in life. Ask and you shall receive.

Reasons to Go Within—Personal Application

Coaching Questions:

1. Answer the list of five questions labeled Important Questions to Ponder in the above Reasoning.
2. What did you discover with your answers?
3. Ask God a question. What is the question? What will you do with the answer?

Guided Meditation I

Imagine you are standing before this beautiful path, a walking path. Maybe it is paved, maybe it is soft green grass, maybe it is a sandy beach but it is a defined path. You are urged from within to walk it. You step onto it, you know this is where you are to be, yet you don't know exactly where it is taking you. You notice a beautiful lamp on your left side. It is not lit. You ask the question:

- What is my purpose? Then the light begins to shine from the lamp.
- You go a few more steps and another beautiful lamp shows up, this one on your right side. You ask the question, do I

have a choice in all the decisions of my life? The light shines brightly.

- As you walk this path, you see another lamp; this one is right in front of you. Ask the question, who do I think God is? The light becomes brilliant and colors burst forth and dance around you.
- As you continue down your path, you see two lamps, one on each side. You ask the questions, who do I believe I am and who do I believe everyone else is? The two lamps light up and streams of light connect the two lamps and then enfold you in light.

You hear the words from within saying "Thy word is lamp under my feet light in my heart." You know you are free to ask the questions as within are the answers.

Meditation II

Close your eyes, breathe gently and lovingly into your body. See the air that is filling your body, know this is coming from the Infinite, full of the knowledge, the wisdom, the understanding of all the mysteries of the universe. It is flooding each cell with this life giving oxygen. Oxygen assists us in helping us to think clearly, to breathe, to live, to think, to feel, to discern.

We are connected to Spirit through the air we breathe. It is the energy around us. We are connected to Spirit through our mind. Your mind created in partnership with the Divine mind live as one. We are connected to Spirit through our heart. Heart to Heart. Each beat of our heart connects us to our Creator. And the two become one, beating in unison. All wisdom, all knowledge, all understanding, all discernment dwell within. All knowing, perceptions are within.

Now see a gold thread shimmering and light filled coming from the top of your head to the energy source in your forehead. The thread stops at the spinning deep blue light in the middle of your forehead. Now see the gold thread staying connected to your third eye move down and connect to your heart. So here is this shimmery, gold thread coming from the top of your heart connected to your third eye and continuing down to your beautiful emerald heart center. Divine mind is now connected to Divine intuition is connected to Divine love.

All discernment, all answers are found when these three centers are connected. You are now energetically connected to the Source of all guidance.

Ask of it what you will. What is it that you need to make a decision about? What is it that you need to release in order to move forward? Where is the judgment that is about others? Where are you stuck and need Divine Intervention/Discernment? What story or belief are you holding on to that may be blocking discernment? Where is your ability to be compassionate fading? What would give you peace right now?

Let Divine Mind, Divine Intuition and Divine Love instruct you.

All wisdom, understanding, knowledge and discernment are yours for they are Gifts of the Spirit.

Acres of Diamonds

Have you ever misplaced something and looked and looked for it and just could not find it? You looked in every place you thought it could be and even in places you didn't think it could be. And then you go back for one last look and there it is, just where you left it. You scratch your head and say, "Where was that when I looked there the last time?" Or maybe you go look in the one place you are sure it would not be and there it is. Or how about the times you have looked for something, did not see it and then someone finds it and says "If it were a snake it would have bitten you."

We all have had those times, haven't we? It can be a pretty frustrating experience. What if it were something so valuable, so precious that you think I <u>must</u> find it? You seek and search for it but you just can't find it because you are looking in the wrong place.

This Reasoning is about following Prosperity Principles. Principles such as:

1. It is already prepared
2. All sufficiency
3. Giving and receiving
4. Forgiveness
5. Oneness
6. Right thinking
7. Gratitude

All of these are principles of creating abundance and prosperity in our lives. I must always begin by saying that Prosperity is not about things, it is about a way of thinking. For all abundance begins with our thoughts, as does scarcity.

I want to share a story with you about a man who had a good life. He had a prosperous farm and did quite well for himself. His crops were always healthy and produced well. His animals were healthy. He had a lovely family and good friends. A traveling monk stopped at his farm for a meal and a nights rest. The monk and the farmer sat by the fire and spoke of many things. They shared their dreams and thoughts. The monk asked the farmer if he was happy and content with his life. The farmer said "Oh yes, I have more than I could ever need. Yes I am content."

The wise sage decided to test this answer and told the farmer this story: He said that this world was once just a bank of fog, (which could very well be scientifically true). He said that the Almighty Creator pushed its finger into the fog and started moving it around, increasing the speed of its moving finger until eventually it whirled that fog into a solid ball of fire. It went rolling through the universe burning its way through the fog until it condensed the moisture and fell into floods of rain that heated and cooled the earth's crust. Then internal flames burst through the cooling crust and made mountains and valleys. This heating and cooling process created first granite, then silver, then gold and finally diamonds.

The farmer was mesmerized by this story of creation. Diamonds he said, "Oh my, they must be the most precious." The monk said "Diamonds are congealed drops of sunlight, most precious." (This is another scientific truth because a diamond is pure carbon actually deposited in sunlight.)

Then the monk said "It is true, diamonds are the last and highest of God's creation, as woman is God's last and highest creation." The monk chuckled and said "I suppose that is why the two have such a liking for each other."

The famer decided right then that he wanted diamonds. When the farmer went to bed that night he went to bed a poor man, not because he had lost anything of material value, but because he was no longer content for what he had but discontent for what he did not have. He had begun his day rich in thought and ended his day in poverty without one change in his physical reality.

He still had a healthy, prosperous farm and all that went with it but thoughts of discontentment made him feel poor. I do not have enough, he thought; I need diamonds.

How many times has that happened to us? We hear or see what others might have, whether it is material things or relationships or gifts and talents and declare ourselves lacking.

Remember p'verty is a way of thinking. One can have very little in material goods and still be rich beyond belief. Just as this famer could have so much and go to bed poor, it is our thoughts that make us content and abundant, not outside trappings.

The story does not end there. The farmer was so discontent, he could not sleep. He tossed and turned and finally he got up and went to the resting monk and said "Wise one, please tell—where can I find the diamonds. I cannot be happy until I have them." Well, everyone knows that when you wake a resting monk, he can be pretty cross. The monk said "Diamonds, that is what you got out of my teaching, you want diamonds so you can be rich?" The reaction of the farmer made the monk sad for the farmer did not hear what the monk was saying. The monk realized that the farmer was not evolved enough to understand.

The monk told the farmer, "The diamonds you are looking for are by a river in a land of abundance where fruits and vegetables are plenty but you will need to understand true poverty before you understand true riches." So the farmer sold his farm, left his family and began his travels to find the land of abundance where a river flows. In his travels he spent all of his money yet had nothing to show for his life, no diamonds, no farm, no family and no friends.

As he aged, he thought before I die I would like to see my farm and family one more time. He found his way back to his farm and when he arrived he asked the owner if could sit by the river. The owner took him down through the abundant fields and sat with him at the river. As they sat the old farmer saw something sparkling through his tears. Then he saw more sparkles as the sun kissed the water. He asked the new owner "What are these?" The new owner responded, "Those are diamonds, they are everywhere by the river."

The old farmer finally got what the monk was trying to teach him. He realized the most precious of God's creation was where he had been, but he did not know it until now. Contentment and riches are in your mind first and then appear in reality. He realized that some of the most important things are right in one's own back yard.

I wonder, have you been searching for something that might be as close to you as you are to yourself? What if you are sitting on acres of diamonds but you can't see them because your thoughts of scarcity or discontentment are getting in the way?

Maybe you think that someone else is much more capable, gifted, smarter or blessed than you. Consequently you go looking for something or someone to complete you or make you more than you are, when you have all you need right inside you.

Earl Nightingale said "Everything that is worthwhile comes to us free—our minds, souls, bodies, hopes, dreams, love, gratefulness, kindness—All priceless possessions that are free." May I add that they are right here in your own backyard. Zig Ziglar said "You can have anything in life you want if you will help enough other people get what they want."

Reasons to Go Within—Personal Application

Coaching Questions:

1. Was there an aha moment for you as your read the story of the farmer and the monk about your own prosperity?
2. Do you believe in the Zig Ziglar principle "You can have everything you want in life if you will help enough people get what they want"?
3. How do you think the above principle works?
4. How did the farmer find enlightenment?

Meditation

Rest and relax in this thought. Everything I want and need is right here and right now. Repeat it to yourself. See it—Feel it—Know it. Everything I want and need is right here and right now.

Rest and Relax in this thought. Everything I need is right here and right now and I am grateful. See it—Feel it—Know it. Everything I want is right here and right now. I am grateful.

Anything I have mistakenly thought I was not—I am, I am more than diamonds, more precious than gold. Before I go looking for it somewhere else, I will remember that it is in me!

Pay It Back or Pay It Forward

The phrase Pay It Forward became popular in the 2000 movie of that name. This phrase was popularized from a novel by Robert Heinlein, *Between Planets* in 1951. It is the concept that a good deed is repaid not to the giver but to another person in need. Paying it back would be repaying a loan. Paying it forward is seeing what was given to you as a gift and it is to be given to another.

Catherine Ryan Hyde wrote a book in the 1950s called *Pay It Forward* in which she suggested with every good deed done to you, you do three good deeds to others. The guideline was that it must be:

1. Something the other could not accomplish on their own
2. The intention of the giver is to make the world a better place

The Heifer Project was created in 1944 with the intention to make the world better and accomplish something that individuals could not accomplish on their own, one cow at a time. This is an example of paying it forward.

Benjamin Franklin described it this way: "I do not pretend to give such a sum; I only lend it to you. When you meet another honest name in similar distress you must pay me by lending this sum to him; enjoining him to discharge the debt in like operation, when he shall be able, and shall meet with another opportunity. I hope it thus go thro' many hands, before it will meet a knave that will stop its progress. This is a trick of mine for doing a deal of good with a little money."

Ralph Waldo Emerson reminded us that "Only seldom do we render benefits from receiving. The benefit we receive is in the rendering them to others." In other words the gift is in the giving not in the receiving. Now, I know we have all heard the St. Francis phrase, "It is more blessed to give than to receive." Acts 20:35. When we pay it forward and the receiver pays it forward and so on and so on, there are only receivers or is it that there are only givers? I think they are one—when you give you receive.

For we are blessed when we give

We are blessed when we receive and then give as was given to us.

Blessing all around

This is a prosperity principle. It is also called the Principle of Reciprocity. Give without expecting and know that all your needs are being met because you give. You are giving because it has been given to you. Many of us are familiar with the Christian scripture teachings regarding giving. II Corinthians 9:7 "Everyone according as was purposeth in his heart, so let him give, not grudgingly or of necessity: for God loves a cheerful giver."

To give just because you wanted to, not because the law said you had to was a completely unheard of thought for the Jewish people of that time. You see Jesus came to free us all from all of the "have to's", the dogma. I find it intriguing that those who believe they are following him are caught up in the have to's and the dogma of their faith.

Luke 6:38 "Give, and it shall be given unto you; good measure, pressed down, and shaken together and running over. For the same measure that you meet with it shall be measure to you again."

Galatians 6:7 "What so ever you sow, you will also reap."

Christian Scriptures are not the only Holy Scriptures that teach this same principle of prosperity and reciprocity.

Hinduism Rig-Veda: "He who gives liberally goes straight to the Gods on the high ridge, he stands exalted."

Bhagavad Gita: "Giving simply because it is right, without thought of return, at the proper time, in the proper circumstance and to a worthy person is enlightened giving. Giving with regrets or expectations of receiving is selfish giving."

Islam Quran: "Those who act kindly in this world will have kindness bestowed on them."

Quran: "You will not attain piety until you expend of what you love, and whatever thing you expend, God knows of it."

Confucianism—Great Learning 10-9 "The accumulation of wealth is the way to scatter people, and letting it be scattered among them is the way to gather the people."

Buddhism—Garland Sutra 21 "Enlightened Beings are magnanimous givers, bestowing whatever they have for the purpose of safe guarding all living beings."

Judaism—Mishnah Abot 4-1 "Who is honored? He who honors others."

Buddhists say that by cultivating generosity in giving we learn the value of being unattached. It has the effect of purifying and transforming the mind of the giver. In the book *The Heart of the*

Buddha by Thich Nhat Hahn, there is a phrase "Giving the Giver." It is another way of saying "pay it forward." "Giving the Giver" is when one gives completely. There is no one looking to watch what is being given, and no one to appreciate how generous one is when one just gives. There is never a problem of running out of resources.

This is one of the Prosperity Principles in action. When using this principle you give because it was given to you. You give because you are grateful. We have every reason in the world to show infinite gratitude to the Universe for everything we have, which is so much. There will never be a way to pay it back to the Infinite, all loving, giving God. So it is not paying back that we do when we give, it is Paying It Forward.

It is Paying It Forward for all future generations. Consider Paying It Forward, Giving the Giver as a way of life, just as you get out of bed each day. You do not have to think, am I going to get up, you just do so. Maybe you wonder why you get up and you may procrastinate, but you do get up.

Consider Paying It Forward, Giving the Giver as a way of life. Instead of expecting to be paid back, pay it forward, instead of expecting someone else to give, Give the Giver.

Giving is not just about money, although that is a big part, but it is your time, your service, your prayers, your love and your kindness.

Give and it shall be given not just to you but to the whole world. That is true prosperity.

When it is all said and done, what better legacy can one leave but to Pay It Forward. To Give as a way of life.

Reasons to Go Within—Personal Application

Coaching Questions:

1. What is the difference between paying it back and paying it forward?
2. Have you ever practiced this principle of reciprocity? You gave someone something and told them when the opportunity arose they are to do the same for someone else?
3. Are you willing to do this in the next week?

Meditation

In this quiet time, in this time of contemplation and reflection, what is it that spirit is whispering to you about? Where are you being called to Pay It Forward? Where have you been blessed and how can you bless others?

With loving gratitude, think of all who have given so much to help make you who you are, doing what you are doing and living life the way you are. This includes our freedom, our education, our spiritual growth. All along the way there were givers in our lives. Give thanks for the givers, the Pay It Forward people in your life. And with that comes a responsibility to give back. To give for all future generations.

Thank yourself for all the giving you give.

To much is given, much is expected.

Affirm your willingness to Pay It Forward and affirm the prosperity in your life.

Section VII

Grace

Grace Introduction

Grace is a small word that says so much. Grace is gratitude. Grace is unchangeable. Grace is forgiveness. To live in a "State of Grace" would be my dream life. In other words, to be so consciously aware of the beauty and wonder ever present that the words that came from my lips continually would be "Thank you, thank you, thank you."

Please steep yourself in the Reasonings in this section. Bathe in the soothing warmth of Grace.

Irresistible Grace

Grace—Grace—God's Grace

Don't you love the sound of the word Grace? Just for a moment close your eyes and repeat the word slowly, Grace—Grace—Grace.

Irresistible Grace is what I am calling this Reasoning. The word irresistible means impossible to defeat or to withstand the force of or the effect of. Now, let's put the word Grace behind the irresistible. Grace means unmerited divine favor given to <u>all</u> with NO EXCEPTIONS. It is also thought of as a honor bestowed upon us that requires nothing to be earned or favor to be returned.

Irresistible reminds us that nothing can block it. Nothing, nothing can stop Grace!

Romans 8:35 "Who shall separate us from the love of Christ? Shall trouble—hardship, persecution—danger, swords?"

Aramaic Bible—"What will separate me from the love The Messiah suffering or imprisonment, persecution or famine or nakedness, or peril, or sword? Nothing in all these things we are more than conquerors. Neither death nor life, nor angels, nor rulers, nor things present, nor things to come, nor power, nor height, nor depth, nor anything else in all creation can separate us from the love of God" or <u>Grace</u>. God and Grace are synonymous.

Rumi, our Sufi master poet, put it this way:

> "Be like the sun for Grace and Mercy.
> Be like the night to cover others' faults.

Be like running water for generosity.
Be like death for rage and anger.
Be like the earth for modesty.
Appear as you are. Be as you appear."

Grace cannot be contained or stopped. Grace is the song of the universe. It is the appearance of the sun, the night, the water, the earth. No one escapes Grace. You can be a believer or not. You are still living in a state of Grace, meaning unmerited, unearned favor and love. You have been bestowed with it and you can never earn it or repay it. <u>That is the state of Grace!</u>

I have asked the following question: "Is there room in Spiritual teachings for the word undeserving as a principle?" I continue to ponder that question. My answer at this point has come to one word, Grace. There is no undeserving or deserving, it is all Grace.

Have you ever heard this phrase or maybe you can recall a time when you said it yourself; "But by the Grace of God, there I go." This phrase is often used to imply that someone is in a low place; down and out would be another way to say it. The implication is that Grace is what keeps us from being there, right? What is wrong with that thought? It says that the other is not living in a state of Grace—Grace left him/her. Does that sound right? How could that even be?

Grace speaks of an all-encompassing energy that never leaves. It may come in many forms but always present, never earned. Whether we are using Grace as a noun or a verb it has the same beauty and energy. Grace as a noun: charm, ease, elegance, loveliness, kindness, consideration, compassion, forgiveness, mercy, blessing, prayer, thanksgiving, generous, goodwill. Grace as a verb: dignify, elevate, enhance, favor, glorify, honor, adorn, beautify.

When I think of Grace I see it as living in a state of being that has nothing to do with me but has everything to do with living under the divine, sacred influence of the most high.

Psalm 91 says it this way: "You who lives in the shelter, secret place of the most high who abides in the shadow of the almighty." This shadow when present is Grace.

One needs this Grace according to the Hindu faith to achieve spiritual self-realization. The difference between Grace from a Christian perspective and a Hindu one is the Hindu faith often suggests that Grace is not a free gift from God but rather must be earned by selfless service.

And from the Islam faith it is recorded that Muhammad once said that "None amongst you can get into Paradise by virtue of deed alone, not even I, but that Allah should wrap me in his Grace and Mercy."

In other words good intentions and deeds are not enough if you lacked Grace. Whatever anyone believes about the purpose for Grace, the fact seems to remain that Grace is present and is here to divinely influence our presence on earth. Many of us are familiar with what has come to be known as the Serenity Prayer.

> God grant me the serenity to accept the things I cannot change
> The courage to change the things I can
> And the wisdom to know the difference.   Reinhold Niebuhr

My understanding is that when Reinhold Niebuhr originally wrote that prayer it sounded this way:

"God give us Grace to accept with Serenity the things that cannot be changed, courage to change the things that can and the wisdom to distinguish one from the other." I like that version because it acknowledges the power is in the Grace and the Grace is always present without pause, without a price. It is the gift from the Infinite for all.

If Grace is this ever present, ever free energy that when used as a noun is ease, charm, compassion, generosity, good will, forgiveness, mercy and when used as a verb is to dignify, elevate, enhance, honor and glorify our presence on this earth, then aren't we blessed people to have this ever presence within our being?

How we show up in the ever present inclusive energy field of Grace is ours to own.

Because of Grace we breathe, we live, we love, we laugh, we serve, we create, we have the capacity to beautify and adorn the world with gratitude. There is a reason we call the mealtime prayer Grace. We are grateful. We are graceful.

So it is!

Reasons to Go Within—Personal Application

Coaching Questions:

1. What is your definition of Grace?
2. Do you believe one can "Fall from Grace"?
3. How do you demonstrate Grace in your life?

Meditation:

This is our time to open our hearts and minds to messages meant just for you from the Infinite, Grace Giver. This is always made a little easier in silence and sometimes more powerful in the presence of other graceful spirits. I ask you to whisper the word GRACE a few times. Feel the vibrations in your body as you say the word Grace—Grace. Just whisper it in the beginning and then if you are comfortable, say it a little louder, Grace—Grace—Grace. As we join in the energy and vibration of acknowledging the presence of Grace, what would your life look like if you were more aware of the Grace that is ever present? How will you choose to use the energy of Grace in your life this week?

Living in Grace

What does "Grace" mean to you? If you were living in a constant state of Grace, what would be different in your life? These are the questions I asked myself as I prepared this Reasoning. As you read this, ask yourself these questions as your answers may be different than mine.

Grace from Webster's Dictionary means seemingly effortless movement—an elegance, beauty, smoothness of form and movement. Generosity of spirit, to forgive, a capacity to accommodate.

WOW—We don't have to go too deep into the religious or spiritual thought to see the magnificent energy of GRACE!!

Gracious means merciful, kind, benevolent, compassionate, tender. From the Latin: Grace means unmerited or undeserving favor, can't be earned but is freely given.

When John Newton, the captain of a slave ship came face to face with his fear of death and his even stronger fear of coming face to face with his God as his ship was being tossed to and fro on a treacherous sea, the possibility of amazing grace became ever apparent. He promised God that if God spared his life he would change his life. He wrote "Amazing Grace, how sweet the sound that saved a wretch like me" after this incident.

Many have changed the word wretch to Soul, but if we understand that those words were written as a testimony to God's love, wretched is what John Newton felt when he saw his life as a slave trader next to the infinite merciful love of God. He lost fear and gained Love.

In that moment he became aligned with that infinite love. Grace is knowing our alignment with Infinite Love. Christian thought says Grace is something made possible by God through Jesus Christ. Hindu thought infers that Grace is not so much a gift, it needs to be earned through devotion. Buddhist thought—Grace isn't automatically given but only as the disciple is ready for it. Which in effect is not grace at all—this is likely a major difference between Christianity and Buddhism.

Kabir (1440-1518), the Indian Poet wrote about Grace.

> "In your heart, grace exists
> Are you looking for me, says Grace, my shoulder is next to yours
> What is God, what is Grace, the breath inside the breath
> If you don't see, touch, know Grace, what is the use of the
> name, God?"

Grace is the smooth, breathless, movement of Spirit. It is God moving through you as you move through life.

Grace is like the wind; you can't see it, but you know it is there by the movement of the leaves on the tree, the flag waving from a pole, your hair in your face as the breeze goes by. Ramakrishna said: "The winds of Grace are always blowing, but we must raise our sails."

These quotes speak so much to me. Grace is always present but if I don't participate I will not move through life with that smooth effortless ease that comes from the Spirit. The Spirit of compassion is accommodating, tender, kind, benevolent and always graceful. Like a sailboat with the sails raised high and the gentle breeze moving it across the lake effortlessly. Grace is knowing our alignment with the infinite flow of life, of love.

What would your day be like if you awoke in the morning and before you even opened your eyes, you acknowledged the presence of Grace, your alignment with the infinite flow of life and love?

As you move through your day with an effortless, elegant ease like that sailboat with her sails up, you are conscious of the presence of the energy of Grace, kind, benevolent, compassionate, forgiving, tender ever present love, Grace.

As you close your eyes to go to sleep you whisper the words, Grace, Grace, Sweet, Sweet Grace. You drift off to sleep with the sound of Grace on your lips. Grace is the knowing that you are aligned with the infinite flow of divine love.

Grace cannot be limited to a blanket definition, that is not the nature of Grace. Grace is a personal experience with a knowing that supports and sustains every moment of every day.

For Captain John Newton, Grace was his awareness that Infinite Love was his no matter what he did. His personal story about Grace was that it changed his life.

For the Sufi poet Kabir, Grace is the breath within the breath. It is knowing the presence of God in his heart.

For Ramakrishna, Grace is like the wind blowing on this human vessel, moving us across the seas of life.

Marianne Williamson speaks of Grace as the mystical power of our own inner resources that lays the foundation to live our chosen path.

Grace can be the Synchrodivinity that appears to remind us that a Higher Source is guiding our lives. Grace can be those spiritual guideposts that navigate us.

Grace can be the ability to see God in everyone you meet.

Grace can be the silence of a quiet mind.

Grace can be the expression of Gratitude.

Lean back into the arms of Grace, letting go, letting God.

Surrendering to all possibilities unlocks and opens up the door to Grace.

As Anne Lamott said "Maybe we don't ever need to understand the mystery of Grace—only that it meets us where we are but does not leave us where it found it."

Reasons to Go Within—Personal Application:

Coaching Questions:

1. If you were living in a constant state of awareness of Grace, how would your life be different?
2. What do you suppose your day would look like if before you opened your eyes in the morning, you acknowledged the presence of God's Grace in your life?
3. What if you went to sleep with Grace—going to sleep with Grace as the last word on your lips?
4. How do you feel Grace?

Meditation

Breathe the breath within the breath. I am open and receptive to the energy of Grace in my life now.

In this sacred, Grace filled moment, look within for your understanding of Grace. What does Grace look like for you? Is it a leaf blowing gently across the ground, dancing with each burst of wind? Is it the gentle moving clouds against an azure blue sky. Is it a smile, a look that says you are loved? Is it a butterfly landing on a flower?

Go into meditation whispering the words Grace, Grace, Grace and let it take you to a sacred, sacred, sacred place.

Section VIII

Angels

Angels Introduction

For some this may be an odd section to include in *A Voice of Reason*. As you read more of my personal journey you may have a deeper understanding. The fact is that one half or more Americans believe in angels. I begin this section with some statistics from a survey released by Baylor University to set the stage for the next three Reasonings on angels. This section invites you to open yourself to the possibilities of angels being around you. Have fun!

Half of Americans believe in angels

Half of all Americans believe they are protected by guardian angels, one-fifth say they've heard God speak to them, one-quarter say they have witnessed miraculous healings, 16 percent say they've received one and 8 percent say they pray in tongues, according to a survey released by Baylor University.

The wide-ranging survey of 1,648 adults, who were asked 3550 questions on their religious practices last fall, reveals a significant majority who are comfortable with the supernatural.

Have you thought about where you stand on the topic of angels?

Is this something that you can share, talk about, reveal to others? Or is this a topic that you must keep to yourself?

This next section reveals angels in history as well as personal experiences of people just like you and their situations of encountering angels. Could a 6 year old child talk to an angel? Could an angel assist in changing a car tire? Do you have a guardian angel? All of this will be looked at (investigated further) in these next few pages.

Entertaining Angels Unaware

Hebrews 13:1-2—"Let mutual love continue. Do not neglect to show hospitality to strangers for by doing that some have entertained angels without knowing it."

Can you imagine that you may have entertained or been in the presence of an angel and you did not know it?

Last year after having my tire blow out on the toll way while going 65 miles per hour, I was carried across three lanes of fast moving trucks to safety on the right side shoulder of the expressway. A large African American male in a black Cadillac ministered to me by changing my tire and following me for 20 miles to make sure I was in good shape to continue my journey home. I believe he was one of my angels.

After hearing my story of this event, a friend of mine shared an incident similar to mine while she was coming back from Toronto. An African American man helped her address her car trouble on her journey home.

A bit later another friend told me of another similar experience but in this case the man appeared to her while her son was in the hospital. At this time she was feeling alone and in need. Is this coincidence or were there angels ministering to us, protecting us?

Angel means messenger from God or protector.

Hebrews 13:1-2. "Do not neglect to show hospitality to strangers for by doing so some have entertained angels without knowing it." It is one of the things I believe I am doing by opening up my home for entertaining. I <u>have</u> entertained many angels.

Psalm 112-1 "Praise ye the LORD. Blessed is the man that feareth (respects) the LORD, that delighteth greatly in his commandments."

This is just another reason to choose mutual love and hospitality. It is saying that we all are divine beings just as Christ was.

When I lived in downtown Chicago I was often approached by street people—the homeless. This verse would come to mind. I would wonder, is this a little Christ in disguise? I would often look in their eyes and try to find the answer. Many times I would feel a strong message to give them the leftovers of my meal or to go the closest store to provide food.

Once a man washing car windows declined to take money for his effort, he just responded "No thank you, God is with you!" There are angels among us and we are to be kind and show love.

Hebrews 12:21,22 (Moses speaking): "I tremble with fear. But you have come . . . to the city of the Living God . . . and to innumerable angels."

So, this says we are in the company of innumerable angels; they are all around us!

Dr. Carl Jung said, "Angels personalize a coming into a consciousness of something that is new arising from deep within our unconscious." So, if we interrupted the verse metaphysically may we be mindful to allow our thoughts to rise to a new level of consciousness. Never let your divine heavenly awareness be sent away with our provisions. It could be a reminder of our connection and responsibility to the heavenly realm.

What would it mean to allow your thoughts to rise to a new level of consciousness that would let you go deeper? Thoughts being the angels and your willingness to provide a welcome place being the entertainment.

How many times have you had an amazing thought yet you never entertained that thought long enough to allow it to create something divine?

Whether they are heavenly beings disguised as earthlings or earthlings with the spirit form of Christ, there is wisdom. Be gracious for you do not know what can come from that graciousness.

Coincidence or angels?

The book of Hebrews, thought to be authored by Paul, speaks of angels more than any other book in the Bible. We know that the New Testament was written after Jesus died, somewhere between 30 and 70 years after his death. We also know that much of the early writings were not included in the version of the Bible most of us know. The Gnostic Gospels have only recently been acknowledged.

Be aware that you may be in the presence of angels—earthly or heavenly. They come to remind us of their presence of the divine.

Archangels/Archetypes

Psalms 91:11—"The Lord will command his angels to guard you in all your ways."

Since I have shared my message on angels, more people have told me their angel stories. A friend mentioned an African American man in a trench coat who appeared to her during a dark moment and reminded her to look up. A New Thought music composer and performer told me of a time when she was lost and not feeling safe. An African American man in a Cadillac who was wearing a long coat came to her rescue and gave her the message that he would lead her to her destination. My African American angel came to my assistance in a Cadillac assuring me that I would be taken care of. There is Synchrodivinity in the fact that all three of us have had an African American angel.

My Administrative Assistant Sal shared with me that during an angel meditation he discovered that one of his angels was a butterfly and since then he has seen butterflies in many places. I know there are angel stories all around that can be shared. Please feel free to share your angel stories with me at avoiceofreasonbook.com.

Angels seem to be some kind of mysterious phenomenon that has captured the curiosity of wisdom seekers and religions as well as artists, musicians and psychologists. All religions have stories and icons about angels.

In the world of psychology, Dr. Carl Jung contributed so much in the area of understanding our connection to all. He recognized the concept of our oneness, a form of collected unconsciousness, universally experienced by all, yet often hidden in the unconscious.

Dr. Jung is credited in modern psychology with Archetypes. St. Augustine spoke of an Archetype called the IMAGO DEI or Image of God that is imprinted in every living being.

This message suggests that our spiritual journey here is to make the God image dominant in our core personality and weave all other archetypical aspects under this image of God.

Jung believed as do many others that there are numerous archetypes or aspects of our psyche. The main four according to Jungian thought are:

1. The Shadow—Our dark or troubled side
2. The Anima—Masculine
3. The Animus—Feminine
4. The Self-Divine—The real God aspect

According to Dr. Jung, our spiritual, emotional, psychological journey here on earth is to make our Divine Archetype the most present, dominant conscious aspect of our being.

Angels are Archetypical characters. They are expressions of the Divine—aspects of the most holy.

St Thomas of Aquinas said: "An angel can illumine the thought and mind of man by strengthening the power of vision and by bringing within his reach some truth which the angel himself contemplates."

I believe understanding more of the angelic realm can only help us understand more of our own divinity. Also, we can use all the help available. Anything that can bring us into more consciousness or awareness of the Sacred, the Divine, the High or Real Self is a good thing.

The following information is composed from those who study archangels. Most people can name a couple of the archangels. There are believed to be seven archangels and they come from the 8th choir. In order to make some sense of what appears to be a holy mess, a hierarchy was created. Somewhat like our own planetary system, nine celestial orders (choirs) orbiting around the throne of Glory—The Source of everything, God.

Archangels are in the 8th orbital ring. All the different angels originate from these orbital levels—Cherubim's, Seraphim's, Powers, Dominions, Principalities, Virtues, Thrones and Archangels. This business of angels can be very sophisticated and quite intriguing as is our own psyche. Archangels seem to be most accessible to our understanding. Maybe because their names came from scriptures and they have specific responsibilities. Generally the thought is that there are seven, although Islam only recognizes four. Michael, Gabriel, Raphael and Uriel are the four archangels that seem to be most familiar.

1. Michael—means "Who is as God." This would be the Jungian archetype. The Self—The Divine nature within. Michael is named in the book of Daniel and in Revelations. It is thought that it was Michael who was in the Burning Bush that appeared to Moses. The I AM. He held Abraham's sword back when offering Isaac. Michael usually is shown with a sword, thought of as the Sword of Truth. Also in his left hand you see scales that represent justice or balance. This is the symbol often used in our legal system. We can call forth Michael to help understand the truth of our Being, our Divine Self, to bring Balance into our Being.
2. Gabriel—It is thought that Gabriel is the only female in higher echelons of angels. She is the only angel other than Michael mentioned by name in the Old Testament. Gabriel

appeared to Daniel to tell him of the coming of a Messiah. She came to Zacharias to tell of the coming of John the Baptist. She came to Mary to announce the coming of Jesus. According to Joan of Arc, it was Gabriel who persuaded the Maid of Orleans to help the Dauphin. She would be the archetype of Animus, the feminine side of our psyche. She is the feeling, birthing aspect. When we need guidance in regards to our purpose or creativity, we can call on the archangel Gabriel.

3. Raphael—His name means "The Shining One Who Heals." Rapha means healer or doctor. Often he is associated with the image of a serpent and fish. Our modern medical symbol has a snake entwined in the motif. Raphael is especially fond of travelers, the Tobit. He assists in the healing of wounds, both physical and emotional. We can call forth Raphael to aid in our healing process.

4. Uriel—Means "Fire of God." Uriel is the least known of the four major archangels. Archetypically he could be seen as the threshold guardian. Uriel is considered a Righteous Angel— in that he is not so soft and that is how we perceive most angels. When Jacob wrested with an angel, the strongest candidate for that position is Uriel. Uriel is the dark angel. Maybe our shadow archetype? Uriel was thought to be the one with a sharp eye warning Noah of the floods. When we need strong, righteous, keen-eyed support, Uriel might be the archangel to call upon.

I love angels because they remind us we are not alone on our spiritual journey. They remind us of protection and guidance. Dr. Carl Jung said that angels personify—"The coming into consciousness of something new arising from the deep unconscious." In other words, our angels help us connect with our God nature.

Maybe you have seen or felt an angel and then wondered if the angel was real. If our thoughts create, we have created a healing, loving energy that is as real as it gets.

According to Hebrew, Islam, Christian legend or lore, there are nine heavens or nine choirs, seven archangels, nine celestial orders orbiting the throne of glory similar to our planetary system. This can be thought of as a universe of its own. Choirs closer to the center commune more directly with divinity and receive unfiltered illumination. There are nine circles that move from the center. Each are called choir.

The 1st choir—Seraphim—Holy, Holy, Holy is the Lord of Hosts, they affirm and sing the song of creation and celebration. Their primary vibration is love. It appears as two faces and six wings.

The 2nd choir—Cherubim—The primary vibration is knowledge. It appears as four wings and four faces. Over time this magnificent being has been shrunk to chubby little wing babies and I for one will never understand this transformation.

The 3rd choir—Thrones express divine will through waves of creativity. Archangel Raphael could be the leader.

The 4th choir—Dominions are sometimes known as the fire speaking angels. They regulate angels duties and are channels of mercy.

The 5th choir—Virtues are the angels who bestow blessings on high usually in the form of miracles or heroes.

The 6th choir—Powers are supposedly the first angels created by God. They are the border guards who patrol heavenly pathways.

Romans 13:1, Paul says "The Soul is subject to the powers." So it seems to be their job to balance our shadow side.

The 7th choir—Principalities are the protectors of religions. They are very busy angels I would say!

The 8th choir—Archangels are generally referred to as the chief or leading angel and are the most frequently mentioned throughout the Bible.

The 9th choir—Angels are the angels closest to the material world and humans. They deliver the prayers to God and God's answer as well as other messages to the humans. They are caring and assist those who request help.

Angels Among Us

Psalm 91:11—"For He will command His angels concerning you to guard you in all your ways . . ."

A prayer I have often said is the following:

> The light of God surrounds me
> The love of God enfolds me
> The power of God protects me
> The presence of God watches over me
> Whenever I am, God is and all is well!
>
> ~ James Dillet Freeman

I am sure that most, if not all of us have had experiences in our lives when we knew there was a Power, a Presence that you may not have understood, but you knew it was watching over you, guiding you and enfolding you.

Angels have always been a part of my awareness. Long before anyone ever taught me Bible stories, there was a knowing that I had protectors and guides, that I was never alone. I had my first verbal communication with an Angel when I was around six years old.

My freedom to share this story came from one of those signs I often speak of. Reading Michael Beckwith's *Spiritual Liberation*, on the first pages he encourages us to share out loud spiritual revelations, not to hide them but to bring them forward in life and share.

I would like to say that my encounter demonstrated some great prophesy or deep mystical experience, the stories that legends are made of, but no, it was an ordinary communication spoken to me from the top of an apple tree. Well, if you call talking to a figure about eight inches tall that seemed to float ordinary, then it was ordinary. What the angel who introduced herself as Anna said, made sense to me as a six year old. Any adult might say, "Why would an angel ever say something like that?" Well it took me years to get the full depth of her words, but I did get it. Some say children and animals are able to see angels and guides because of their pureness. They have not been filled with doubt about the existence of angels.

Here is my story: When I was not much older than age six I had my first known encounter with an angel. The story I am about to share has been a puzzle for me for most of my life. As I have grown older I have learned how to apply metaphors to the things in my life that I don't understand. With this I have more clarity regarding the message that the angel delivered, but there are still questions.

I take you back to a warm, summer day. I had just come home from dance class. It was during the ½ mile walk home that I began dreaming of those tiny green apples just waiting for me. I could just see myself climbing up my favorite apple tree with my salt shaker tucked in my pocket. Oh, my mouth was watering. I ran in the house, said a quick "hi" to my mom in passing and rushed to change my clothes so I could make my dream come true. My mom called to me and said "Sherry Ann, I just heard from Mrs. Stack" (that was our neighbor who had 13 kids) "She said those little green apples will make you very sick and give you a bad tummy ache. So, no more eating little green apples."

You could have put a knife to my heart. I love little green apples. I always ate little green apples. I never got a stomach ache. What did that Mrs. Stack know anyway? Just because she had 13 kids did not mean she knew me and my tummy. As I walked through the kitchen with a feeling of forlorn, I slipped the salt shaker in my pocket. My mom said to me from the living room, "Remember, no eating those apples Sherry Baby."

"Yes Mama" I replied.

Well, I climbed up my apple tree and I perched myself on my favorite limb and there it was, the perfect green apple, not too big, not too little, not too green and no worm holes. Now I tried to be a good girl but this was just too much for one little girl who loved green apples to bear.

Looking down at my salt shaker and up at the apple, I felt I was making a serious life altering decision. I remember feeling tears run down my face. I wanted to be a good girl obeying my mom. I also did not believe because Mrs. Stack said so, that I could not eat my apples.

How many times in life are we told that we must believe in things that go against our knowing? How many times have we believed lies because we trusted the source?

Well just about that time, a little blonde angel appeared. She had no wings but I knew she was an angel because I asked her: "Who are you?" She said: "My name is Anna; I am your angel. I have a message for you." I could not believe my ears. These things do not just happen, do they? Apparently they do!

Anna said her message was: "Little green apples will never give you a stomach ache, follow your heart." That was all she said and then she was gone. Now that message might not seem so profound to you but for a six year old girl who did not want to disappoint her mom but yet still trust her own heart, it was one of the most profound messages of my life. Because of that message from my angel, I do not believe in things just because people say it. Because of Anna I believe in supernatural spiritual beings in my life. Because of that message I follow my heart more often. This is one of reasons I often preface the signing of my name with "From My Heart."

I was so impressed as a child that I had my very own angel, when I gave birth to my daughter, I named her Angel. Angel means messenger from God. My daughter Angel was a messenger from God which changed my whole life. When I discovered she was coming I began a journey of understanding what it means to love from a deep place, to understand love as giving more than taking, of contributing to the development and growth of another. It is to understand the circle of life.

My daughter Angel became a guardian angel to animals; she is their protector. That is one form of an earth angel. Earth angels dedicate their life to a purpose of healing, helping, protecting and affirming others. We can all be angels of an earth form. Each time you demonstrate your Christ nature you are demonstrating your angelic nature. You are a messenger from God.

There are earth angels and heavenly angels. Doreen Virtue's books on angels will give you more education on this subject.

There are also angels of a heavenly being, like Anna in my apple tree. A recent survey conducted by Baylor University said that more than half of Americans believe they are protected by guardian angels. 25% said they have witnessed miraculous healings as a result of angelic visits. I suspect that the percentage is even higher. Nevertheless, many of us know there are heavenly beings called angels.

There are many books written by angel experts. What exactly makes one an expert, I am not sure. Angels and spirit guides are often called our Invisible Helpers, sometimes made visible. From a religious historical perspective, they are ancient. The oldest illustrated depiction of an angel is 6000 years old.

We know a large amount of early Christian material was excluded from the Bible. Much of the apocryphal gospels were excluded which contained many references and a great deal of information on angels. *Three Books of Enoch*, from 2nd century BC and the Bible as we know it mention angels 300 times.

The Old Testament speaks of communication and visits from angels. The two angels that were given names were Michael and Gabriel. The New Testament refers to the seven churches as each having their own angel. Martin Luther said: "An angel is a spiritual creature created by God without body for the service of Christendom and of the church."

One of my favorite scripture references is Psalms 91:11, it is my life Bible verse: "He will command His angels concerning you to guard you in all your ways."

Hebrews 13:2: "Let brotherly love continue. Be not forgetful to entertain strangers for there by some have entertained angels unawareness." Maybe this is why I enjoy hosting people in my home because it feels like I am filling my home with enumerable angels.

Hebrews 12:22: "We are in the company of enumerable angels." Early Jewish teachings speak of each of us having 11,000 angels.

I hope the above message gave you a sense of the love, guidance and protection that is all around you ALWAYS. I encourage you to not be afraid to call on your angels and guides to guide you.

Synchrodivinity and the signs will continue to come to us from Spirit. Angels can bring you these signs.

Reasons to Go Within—Personal Application

Coaching Questions:

1. Have you ever had an encounter with an angel?
2. If so, how did it impact your life?
3. What other meanings could be attributed to the message I received from my angel Anna? Is it ok to eat little green apples?

Sherry's Calling All Angels Meditation:

Breathe gently and slowly, allowing your body to sink into the space of comfort and relaxation. In this meditation join me in setting the intention of communicating with an angel, your guardian angel. Trust whatever awareness comes up for you and allow the power of imagination to flow during this time with the angelic world. Everything that has ever been created came from imagination; all that has sprung forth is from the imagination of God. Imagination, possibility, angels are just words for God, Good, Creation, Sacred, Divine, Source.

Let's begin by thinking of a color. The color that comes to your mind will be the color your Guardian Angel will identify to you in your presence. Trust your color choice. Visualize that color as a small pinpoint of light within your heart. Let the light grow larger until it fills your whole heart, your chest, and let it continue moving through your body until it fills you whole being. From the top of your head to the soles of your feet, you are filled with this color. The energy and purity of this color fills the room. Just as your angel's love and presence fills you. Knowing your Guardian Angel is here and its presence is being affirmed in this color. I now want you to focus your attention on your angel's form even though in pure energy essence angels may have no gender or form. They often appear in gender or form knowing you might need to be supported in that form. So sense within you, whether your angel has a gender, a form, a body. Once the thought comes, trust it. Affirm my angel is . . . . My angel comes to me in the color of . . . . and in this form . . . . If what comes to you is a feeling, affirm the angelic feeling, my angel comes with this feeling.

Now ask yourself the name you would give your guardian angel. Just trust whatever name imagination gives. It is the right name. Know that angels appreciate being named by you. Affirm your angel's color, your angel's gender or form or spirit and your angel's name. I affirm my angel is golden. She is feminine and her name is Anna. Her energy is truth. Whisper your angel's color, gender, energy and name.

Welcome your guardian angel. Know that your angel is always present and available to you. "For he (God) will order his angels to protect wherever you go. They will hold you up with their hands so you won't even hurt your foot on a stone." Psalms 91:11,12 (NLT)

You may ask your guardian angel a question if you wish or you may just want to listen for your angel to speak. Thank your power of imagination to bring forth this experience, to allow a space where you and your angel can meet. Maybe you have met many times; maybe this is your first meeting. Affirm the two of you will meet again.

Section IX

Sacred Thoughts about our Creator

Sacred Thoughts about our Creator Introduction

This is the ninth section and the last in *A Voice of Reason*. As I expressed in the introduction of this book, this content was not originally written to be a book, but it is a collection of my wanderings, searching and discoveries into possibilities. I needed a Policy Manual for my life. There are stacks and stacks of notebook paper filled with more thoughts. I am sure they will continue to mount and maybe some will end up in future books. There is always a driving factor for me to know the Infinite. Knowing the Infinite is not static, it is a fluid, changing energy.

This section is a glimpse into my constantly ever changing mind. The mind that is always seeking to know God. The God I know is not necessarily the God you know at this moment but it is all God. I hope you enjoy this thought provoking process to assist you in knowing your God.

Religion and Spirituality—Strange Bedfellows

George Clooney spoke at the Global Telethon Fundraiser, Hope for Haiti to raise funds for the earthquake victims. He said: "At the core of every religion is the belief that we care for everyone." What do you think about that? Do you believe that at the core of every religion there is a caring for everyone?

I suppose one would need to define "Caring" to ultimately answer that question because if caring means nonjudgmental acceptance, then I cannot buy that it is the foundation of Religion. The foundation seems to be more about who is right. It is difficult to embrace that the foundation of religion is caring when throughout history religious organizations have waged "Holy Wars." I cannot accept that churches waging hate and smear campaigns against people can be called caring. I cannot accept that racial and sexual differences can give a religion the right to use free speech, to spread hate and separateness.

George Clooney's words were nice, maybe wishful thinking but I am not so sure they are true. What is true is that the core of <u>Spirituality</u> is to know the oneness of us all, therefore care. "Love thy neighbor as thyself." This all seems to represent strange bedfellows—Religion/ Spirituality is supposed to care for everyone, but doesn't. Spirituality or the search for Spirit often finds us in a religion. If the religion does not honor the journey of seeking spirit then one's spiritual seeking journey either stops there or it leaves religion. According to Webster's Dictionary, Religion's definition is:

- The service and worship of God or a Super Natural
- Devotion to a particular faith
- A personal set of beliefs and practices that matches that faith
- A cause, principle or belief held with faith and ardor

Spirituality does have those aspects but it is not the core. Spirituality's definition focuses on following an inner path of self-awareness, self-mastery, always changing just as we change and the earth changes. The essence of Spirituality is knowing who we really are. It is a bit of a challenge to define more clearly for those who might come to Spirit Space, who we are and what we believe since we do not belong to an already established organized association or religion. We are creating this in a rather organic way and that to me is what Spirituality is—creating from within what connects me to the Infinite.

Spirit Space offers an alternative way to connect with God. We are a small group of rebels and free thinkers gathering together. We are not followers. Are we a church? Are we a faith? What makes us different? We are a non-profit organization filed as an ecclesiastical foundation. Yet we certainly are not a church in the traditional manner. We have no association. We know we are looking for the oneness, yet honoring the differences with a love and a purpose that is so alive and real. It is spiritually grounded in oneness and acceptance. It is grounded in community and in service.

No formal platform has been established. There is no religion or dogma. We have a lot of spirituality!!! I know that anyone would be welcome here, not only welcomed but truly cared for. We are what George Clooney was speaking of, not Religion but Spirituality. We care.

Spirituality is the core; it comes from the inside and flows outward. This outward focus can of course show up in an organized faith. But the caring does not come from being religious; it comes from being connected to the source of love. That source can then be demonstrated in our actions. I know how to live without religion but I do not know how to live without Spirituality.

Gibran, The Prophet said: "Who can separate his faith from his actions or his belief from his occupation? Who can separate his hours before him, saying this is for God and this is for myself, this for my soul and this is for my body?"

Maybe what he was saying is that our actions are our religion. Our actions come from our inward faith or spirituality. Life itself is a sacred, holy adventure! There is a Spiritual Renaissance happening and we are alive and here on this sacred holy adventure. To be spiritually alive is to embrace this world and all of creation with a caring, loving reverence, with kindness.

Hafiz said, "I have learned so much on my journey with God that I no longer call myself a Christian, a Hindu, a Muslim, a Buddhist, a Jew. The truth has shared so much of itself with me that I can no longer call myself a man, a woman, an angel, or even a pure soul. Love has befriended me so completely, it has turned to ash and freed me of every concept and image my mind has ever known." This is Pure Religion.

A while back, I read an article in Body and Soul magazine entitled "How Spiritual Are You?" It was a fascinating read. The article suggests that there are aspects called SQ or spiritual quotient that can be considered as a checklist to determine your SQ. This is a way of assessing your spiritual prayers.

What follows is your spirituality quotient checklist:

1. Ability to sense and act on your connection to the presence of Spirit/God/Love in yourself, others, the world.
2. A tendency to look for the deeper meaning of events, to ask questions that go deeper.

3. A capacity to connect with your inner sense of compassion, peace and awareness.
4. A commitment to some sort of contemplative or meditative practice.
5. A willingness to take responsibility for your own state of mind (peace) regardless of the outer circumstances.
6. Incorporating your intuitiveness to look beyond appearances to see what is important.
7. A knowledge of the oneness /kinship that embraces equality and concern for all of God's creation.
8. Treating feelings of anger, fear, blame and hurt as signals to do self-inquiry and listen to what is behind them.
9. Less afraid to speak the truth and know how to do so gently.
10. Above all, a strong sense of your divine nature.

Notice that many of these points incorporate the Four Agreements by Don Miguel Ruiz.

The Four Agreements are:

1. Be impeccable with your word
2. Don't take anything personally
3. Don't make assumptions
4. Always do your best

When I was personally trying to define Spirituality, what came to me was:

> Religion is looking for God from the outside in.
> Spirituality is seeing God from the inside out.

Be advised that we can easily become as dogmatic as any religion. Rev. Jim Rosemergy said it so well:

"Our God is Love
Our Race is Human
Our Religion is Oneness"

Dr. Carl Jung said: "Some confuse the finger pointing at the moon as the moon." In this case religion is the finger, not the moon. Spirituality is the moon.

Paulo Coelho said: "In the end all religions tend to point to the same light. In between the light and us, sometimes there are too many rules about the light."

What Does God Look Like?

That might seem to be an odd question. Everyone knows what God looks like, right? What?? You don't think you know what God looks like?

We ALL HAVE A CREATED IMAGE, PERCEPTION OF GOD! It is what humans do! We humans even attempt to make God human. Close your eyes for a moment. Say the word God to yourself. What comes to mind for you? What do you see in your mind? What form does God take? Is God coming to you in human form? Maybe God is a wise looking sage or an Indian grandfather. Does the image come with a gender?

Now listen. What do you hear? Does God have a voice? Does God sound like the wind? Like the waves? Is it like someone you know? Does God speak in words? What kind of feelings come up for you as you picture God? Are you comforted or a little uneasy? Can you easily bring God to you and then immediately feel loved?

Whatever thought form that you had about God, you created and more likely than not, your image of God is different than anyone else's. This is what your God looks like!

One of the most important questions of your life, your spiritual life, is: How do you see God? The way you see God will determine the way you see yourself or maybe it is the other way. The way you see yourself will determine how you see God. Whichever way it goes, how you see God will determine how you will see others. The way you see God will also determine how you will treat yourself and others. So let's examine three questions:

1. How do you see God and what does your God look like?
2. Where did that image/template come from?
3. What is truth about God?

These are such important questions. We are made in the image of our Creator yet we are not the Creator.

This message evolved from a book that was given to me and the name of the book is *The Shack* by William P Young. The story begins with a tragedy. The event was so painful, it was difficult to read. I just wanted to wipe it all out and maybe write a new beginning, something not so ugly and devastating. I wanted a story that was much more palatable. Yet sometimes in our journey to knowing God is not always peaceful, perfect and palatable.

One of the main characters is McKenzie Phillips, AKA Mack. Mack, like many of us has a perception of God that was created from his childhood experiences. Often, how we see God is based on how we saw our primary caregivers or adults in our early years of our development. If we see God as male, consider for a moment how you saw your father and/or grandfather.

Those who had a less than positive experience might see God as a male figure with distrust or even with a painful emotional connection. Those who had a loving, positive experience with male authority figures will be much more confident with a male God.

If you had male figures in your life that were critical and/or harsh, you might experience a male God that way. Maybe the figures were distant, unavailable both physically and emotionally. God could seem that way. For many having a male God is just too painful, so it is more comforting to have a female God.

Well, what if the primary females in your early years were the critical ones, more critical or hurtful than males? Chances are you would not be so comfortable with a feminine image of God. There are some who did not get their needs met from their Mother or Father. If they see God in a human form, it is painful, so God often becomes or takes on something of a non-gender role or image, it could be the wind or an animal. So often the image we create of God is based on our childhood experiences.

Remember it is in our humanness we create an image of God. It comes from how we perceived people and events in childhood.

Let's go back to Mack, our main character in the book *The Shack*. His global view of God was not positive. Mack had a father who was very religious, meaning: he went to church, knew all the songs and quoted the Bible. Then he would come home from church, he would get drunk and beat Mack's mother. When Mack was around 13 years old, he attended a revival meeting. He became as they say "Convicted." For you see he felt extremely guilty because he could not protect his mom. He confessed this to a deacon, wanting God to forgive him and help him. This information got back to his father. His less than loving father, got drunk, tied Mack to a tree and beat him while quoting Bible verses.

Now, let's fast forward Mack's life many years later. Mack is a loving husband and father. His family is everything. He made a conscious choice to be the father he never had. He suffered and was haunted from his childhood and there was not much room for God.

Things actually were going along quite well until the horrible event that changed everything. He had no God that could comfort him because what his God looked like was harsh, punishing and could not be trusted. Mack fell into what he called "The Great Sadness." "He wears it like a heavy cloak, draped around his shoulders. The weight of it dulled his eyes and caused his shoulders to slump. Even his efforts to shake it off were exhausting. He ate, worked, loved, dreamed, played in this garment of heaviness, weighed down as if he were wearing a lead bathrobe . . . trudging daily through the murky despondency that sucked the color out of everything." It was truly a Dark Night of the Soul.

Mack had no God of solace and comfort. He only had a God he created from a painful past. His God was a cruel, punishing male that spit Bible verses that wounded his being.

I don't want to give the story away because I want you to read it. But, what happens in this story can blow every image you have of God and the Trinity out of the water. It can open up ideas that could change what your God looks like, sounds like and feels like. But more importantly it can open your spiritual consciousness to unlimited possibilities. What if God were a big black woman called Papa? What if? What if Holy Spirit was a small Asian female with fairy like energy, carrying a small paint brush and a crystal bottle collecting your tears because they are so valuable? They represent our sorrows and our joys. What if?

What if Jesus the Christ were a not so particularly handsome Middle Eastern man that would not stick out in a crowd, but had eyes of compassion that could melt your heart. What if? What if you opened up a hymn book and all references to a male God were removed? What if all references in Scriptures were no longer gender specific? Meaning the songs we sing, the verses we quote would only refer to God—Creator—Beloved—Spirit.

Actually Galatians 3:28 says it like this:

"There is neither Jew nor Greek
Slave nor free
Male nor female
for we are all one in Christ Jesus."

If God Was a Male—If God Was a Female

Isn't that just a curious thought, God being a father or a mother? Is God male or female?

Would you close your eyes for a moment? Imagine you are in the presence of the Divine, creator of all, the source of all that exists, the beginning and end, the I AM. What is this source's gender? What is the gender of God?

I know we humans personalize everything so it should be no great surprise that we personalize even the highest, holiest and unexplained.

Isaiah 55:8 Old Testament Bible: "For my thoughts are not your thoughts, neither are your ways my ways says the Lord. For as the heavens are higher than earth, so are my ways and my thoughts than your thoughts."

It is inconceivable that God has a gender or that God is limited to a form. We have in our nature a need to put everything including God into a mold. What if we did not box in the concept of God? When we place human concepts on God we place human limitations. There is nothing wrong with seeing God as male, or female or both. What I am suggesting is to not be attached to a limitation of the Infinite.

What if that were true in our language, in our thoughts, in our treatment of others? What if that were true in our worship?

What if you went to bed tonight and had a dream so real that it became real in your soul and in that dream you spent three days in a shack with God, Holy Spirit and Jesus and they went completely opposite of every concept you ever had about the Trinity? What if?

Now, I stated in the beginning that we were going to look at these three questions:

1. What does your God look like?
2. Where did that idea come from?
3. What is the Truth?

I will now present Truth. God is Spirit—The **I AM**.

Truth is God, it is not religion

God is not male—God is not female

God is not a noun

The Truth is God is loving, comforting, understanding, healing, giving—God IS. From *The Shack*: "I am a verb, I am that I am. I am alive, dynamic, ever active and moving. I am a being verb."

Scripture says: Isaiah 55:8

> "My thoughts are not your thoughts
> My ways are not your ways declares the Lord.
> As the heavens are higher than the earth
> so are my thoughts than your thoughts"

In other words however you see God, God will always be higher, greater than you could ever imagine. So does the God that you have created in your mind, take you higher? Is your picture of God forgiving, loving and always available? If God is not the God of healing and abundance, is that Really who God IS?

Reasons to Go Within—Personal Application

Coaching Questions:

1. How do you see God and what does your God look like?
2. Where did that image/template come from?
3. What is truth about God?

Meditation

Be still and know that I am God.

I am loving.

Be still and know I am Giving.

Be still and know Peace.

Be still and forgive.

Be still, embrace silence.

Be in the presence of all that IS. The I AM. And so IT IS!

A Message about Lent

In traditional and the orthodox churches the Lenten season is recognized.

Lent is an Anglo-Saxon word for spring. It is derived from a verb meaning to lengthen. This is a time when many practice the giving up or denial of something. For us operating on a different plane, Lent is a season of spiritual growth and stretching, lengthening.

Rather than giving something up such as chocolate or coffee for Lent, knowing these items have no spiritual significance, I suggest that you consider giving up thoughts that do not serve you or your spirit well. If you give something up for Lent, how about if you spend the 40 days giving up something such as judgment, harshness, gossip or negativity. And think of the conversations you will have when someone asks you what you gave up for Lent.

Remember, denial of old thought patterns will often lead you to your own crucifixion.

From Charles Filmore, his Keeping the Lent affirmation: "Forgetting the things that are behind me, I realize: I am strong, positive, powerful, wise, fearless, free spirit, I am God's perfect child. I deny any that says I am not."

Every Thought is a Prayer

My intentions are to explain both from quantum physics (science) and a mystical (spiritual) perspective, the principles working around the idea that "Thoughts Become Things" or some know it as the law of attraction. This is how prayer works.

If each thought actually is a prayer request then we are praying all of the time, aren't we? It has been estimated that we have over 60,000 thoughts a day. WOW. Often our thoughts are random, scattered and ever changing. So God or Universe (I am using them interchangeably) answers all our prayers, then how can any of this make sense to the Universe? Are our 60,000 thoughts prayers?

The first thing to understand is the idea that the Universe only says YES. All requests are answered according to the request. From scripture "God wants to grant us the desires of your heart." Ask, believe and receive.

According to the teachings of Abraham, *Ask and It Is Given* by Esther and Jerry Hicks—When you ask you are given. It is always given. You may respond by saying, "Well, I asked for this or that and I did not get it."

From a quantum physics perspective you have received what you sent out; you just might not have been fully conscious of what you were asking for or that you were even asking.

The Principle Law of Attraction can be a very deliberate intent, conscious or something that is not conscious, yet very present.

For something to be a law—it must happen every time—like gravity—but yet even gravity isn't a law in outer space.

I cannot stress how important it is for all of us to live and operate from a conscious clear awareness. This is what I call being aligned with God, consciousness as it creates an intimacy with the Source. In doing so, we will be more connected to self, our purpose and intention for being. We are made to create and manifest as God does. We were created in God's image with intention. Results improve when we are clearer because our requests and affirmations are clearer.

William James, philosopher, psychologist of the early 1900s said "You are today where your thoughts have brought you, you will be tomorrow where your thoughts take you." That is a sobering thought is it not? "You are today where your thoughts have brought you. You will be tomorrow where your thoughts take you."

We are vibrational beings. Everything in the universe is on a wave frequency. According to Abraham each of us has our own measureable frequency. It is like a receiving mechanism, let's use the example of a radio. When you set your tuner to the station you are going to hear what is playing on that station. Whatever you are focused on is the way you set the tuner; this activates a vibration that becomes a thought sent into the universe.

In 1970, physicists discovered something called the String Theory which describes the universe as tiny vibrating strings of energy. This validated the observations of both the quantum and the traditional worlds of science. The word quantum means "A discrete quantity of electromagnetic energy." Quantum physicists found that what appears to be the solid world is not that at all. It is all energy, vibrations—Energy can express itself as a wave or a particle, sometimes both. We are vibrational beings.

Greg Braden says that "The consciousness of the observer determines how energy will behave." Scientists are just getting this concept. Sages and Wisdom Seekers have known it from the beginning of time. We are all made of energy. The Sanskrit word Chakra means spinning wheel, vibrating. The higher, more spiritual chakras are vibrating at a faster rate than the lower more physical ones. Essentially we are the essence of Spirit. Your Spirit body vibrates at a higher rate than your physical body.

When our thoughts come from a Spiritual place, our intentions will vibrate at a faster speed, not only faster, but clearer, purer. Thoughts become things because thoughts are the precursor to action. The Law of Attraction ends with the word ACTION.

We are responsible for our thoughts; our actions are a reflection of our thoughts. If we say we want a healthy body, we think it but if we do not take ACTION, it won't happen. We are sending a mixed vibration into the universe thereby getting a mixed reaction or answer.

In the Teachings of Abraham, it suggests that the more you focus on a subject, the more active that vibration is. Eventually you will begin to see physical evidence showing up in your experience that matches the essence of the way you have been feeling about the subject you have put all this thought into. This becomes your Emotional Guidance System. Our thoughts, our feelings, our beliefs, our desires and our true nature need to be in alignment and balanced. Being in alignment means you are connected to the truth of who you really are, who God is, the essence of your being is pure, free and perfect. You want the signals you send to be authentic to the thoughts you want to manifest. This is alignment. The simplest way for me to understand how my thoughts become things is by comparing it to a radio. When we turn on a radio and put it on the channel we want to hear, that frequency is sent out into the air waves and is picked up by a frequency that is tuned into that specific channel.

Our thoughts are the channel and when they are sent out, they are picked up by a matching frequency and the thought I sent out is matched to the same universal frequency. The thought, just like the channel I chose on my radio, becomes the program I wanted to hear. If I am not sure which station I want to hear or I have some limiting beliefs that the stations does not exist, I might set the channel in between the two stations and I will not get either station with any clarity. I must be connected to the receiver—God.

The more self-aware we are, the more we can connect to the receiver, the Source. The clearer we are, the more we are vibrating from a spiritual frequency versus a physical frequency. The more we will be in alignment with Spirit. We will be in tune and then our life will demonstrate the principle of Spiritual Manifesting.

This is why affirmative prayer is so powerful and effective. Affirmations, Vision Boards and meditation encourage personal and spiritual development. This is how to reach in to reach out. Life is lived from the inside out. We must go in to go out. Prayer is guiding our thoughts to resonate with the highest good.

Albert Einstein referred to one law which he said contains the sum of all that mathematics and physics have proved true about the universe. He said "This law is a positive force for good and that we tune in on its infallibly perfect workings by the power of thought through prayer."

Eric Butterworth said "Prayer is a technique for achieving unity with God, substance and divine intelligence." The following prayer was written by Eric Butterworth:

"Prayer is not something we do for God but for ourselves.
It is not a position but a disposition
It is not flattery but a sense of oneness
It is not asking but knowing
It is not words but feelings
It is not will but willingness"

Prayer and our thoughts are the meeting place between God and humankind. Prayer connects us with the Divine Mind where all creation begins. The mind has ideas, thoughts and expressions. All manifestations in our world are a result of the ideas we are holding in our mind.

I urge you to align your thoughts, feeling and desires. If there is something you want to manifest. Check to see if there are any mixed intentions. Ask yourself what would it feel like to have it? Ask how would it connect you to God, others, the planet?

Remember, whatever you focus on expands. You get what you send out. Sending love and peace brings love and peace. Try this experiment—Pick a color or a symbol and look for it every day. See if you don't get what you are looking for.

Send good, loving affirmations to yourself and others and see if you don't feel good and loving. Your thoughts are prayers. What have you been praying for lately?

Meditation

In this quiet intimate time, the hearer of all requests and you meet.

What is it you want to manifest in your life?

Know that the universe wants to grant you the highest good. Affirm yes to all good. Thank God for all that is yours to enjoy in the here and now.

Align your thoughts, your feelings and being with the truth of the lightness of your spirit. You are pure spirit, light and energy. Vibrating only good, receiving only good. Your thoughts are pure prayers being heard and being granted. And you give thanks.

The God Within—The God Without

Why pray? Where are we directing our prayers? More than one person has wondered about this. In the New Thought movement this is a topic of interest. What makes us explorers and seekers is our wonderful curiosity, our desire to know and understand our faith. We are not followers, we cannot just accept answers such as "Because we said so." As pilgrims of faith we venture into our hearts and our minds to find answers. Sometimes we discover there is not an answer to be had, we just find more questions. And that is alright too, because as soon as we believe we know, we stop seeking. As Rainer Marie Rilke wrote in his classic *Letters to a Young Poet*, "Be patient toward all that is unsolved in your heart and try to love the questions themselves, like locked rooms and like books that are now written in a very foreign tongue. Do not now seek the answers, which cannot be given you because you would not be able to live them. And the point is, to live everything. Live the questions now. Perhaps you will then gradually, without noticing it, live along some distant day into the answer." Be patient in your heart about all the unanswered questions, for in the questions lie the answer. It is similar to the game of Jeopardy. Look at the question for the answer.

A tradition that has carried over from Unity thought is The Prayer for Protection by James Dillet Freeman. The words are comforting for many of us.

> "The Love of God Enfolds Us
> The Light of God Surrounds Us
> The Power of God Protects Us
> The Presence of God Watches Over Us
> Wherever we are, God IS and ALL IS WELL!"

Many times I have repeated these words. I remember one icy winter day when I was coming back to Michigan from Illinois to lead a Wednesday evening meditation. When I got to Indiana, the roads became a sheet of ice. Cars were pulled over. Trucks were jack knifed every few miles. It was very frightening. One could not get off the freeway because the exit ramps were even icier and all of the ramps had disabled vehicles on them. My hands were frozen to the steering wheel. I avoided putting my foot on the brake for fear of sliding into the truck or car in front of me. The sleet was sometimes blinding. All I could do way say the Prayer of Protection over and over again.

"The Love of God Enfolds Us
The Light of God Surrounds Us
The Power of God Protects Us
The Presence of God Watches Over Us
Wherever we are, God IS and ALL IS WELL!"

There was no praying to the God within. I needed an outside God to help keep my car on the road. This prayer calmed me down and I did arrive safely in Michigan claiming the power of positive affirmative prayer.

I love that prayer. Yet, it is a prayer that is directed to a God outside of our self. The God Without.

Someone once asked me what we are praying to be protected from. In other words, where is the danger or what is the danger? That is a legitimate question, isn't it? What is the Power of God protecting us from? My thought is we are asking to be protected from our thoughts. If our thoughts create, we need to have good thoughts.

I am not sure that is what Mr. Freeman meant, but that is what came to my mind. The reference to the enfolding and the watching over suggests there is a God outside of us. That makes sense to me because something created all the beauty of nature and created us. Yes, we say that our Divine Mind, the Christ Mind, the Buddha Nature, the Infinite Mind exists inside us. "Let this mind be in you which is also in Christ." Philippians 2:5. But we all know our mind did not create the universe. There is a God within and there is a God without. We did not create ourselves so therefore there must be a God outside of ourselves. The idea of God dwelling within, of God living within God's creation is an absolute mystery of the cosmos, is it not?

The purpose of the outside world is to stimulate the experience and the purpose of the inner world is to verify. Without the outside God there is nothing to verify and without the inside God there is no source to find the point of truth that exists in all things. Truth is discovered through the interplay with that which is without and within. Anything that exists within has a physical counterpart. The outside is a reflection of the inside. They are interdependent not independent. Some have thought that as our souls evolve we have less need for physical evidence of God, the outside God. Maybe that is so.

Let's reflect upon the God Within. Luke 17:20, Jesus is speaking, "And when he was demanded of the Pharisees, when the kingdom of God should come, he answered them, The Kingdom of God comes not with observation."

Luke 17:21 "Neither shall they say, lo here! or, lo there, behold, the kingdom of God is within you."

That sounds clear, doesn't it? The Kingdom of God is within, but the translation can also speak of the Kingdom in the midst of you (among you), which implies Within and Without.

The Talmud—Jewish sacred writings suggest: "Live life with your left hand in your pocket, living as if everything depends on God and with your right hand in your other pocket living as if everything is up to you."

I remember sitting in a class on Metaphysics at Unity School of Practical Christianity in Kansas City, MS questioning the idea that there is no God without and that just because God dwells within does not make us God.

There is a difference in calling yourself God and knowing that God dwells within you and that we are an expression of the indwelling God.

The Gnostic Christians of Jesus's time believed to truly know God you must know yourself. The Buddhist teach this same wisdom thought. "To live knowing the God within us is to be connected to the one—the I AM." To live knowing that we are all part of God and that God is greater than and yet dwells within everyone is living the Oneness Principle, the Mystery of God.

John 3:8 describes the mystery like this: "The wind blows where it wishes and you hear the sound of it but cannot tell where it comes from and where it goes. So is everyone who is born of the Spirit." Maybe this is the explanation of the God Within—The God Without. God is like the wind, it blows within and yet we see the wind blowing in the trees and around us—as we see God all around us.

The eastern philosophy can say it in one word, Namaste. I honor this place in you in which the entire universe dwells. I have pondered the idea of a closing prayer that honors the God Within as well as the God Without. All my rough versions to date have not captured the essence of the God Within, the God Without. Maybe there are no words to truly honor our intention because it is such a mystery.

The sacred presence of our Creator is always everywhere and it is most intimately experienced right inside us. May we honor the God Within as well as the God Without.

When we say God and I are one, do we mean we are God?

If a drop of ocean water said, "The ocean and I are one," would you think the drop thought it was the ocean? It is easy to understand that the drop of ocean water and the ocean are inseparable, just as it is easy to understand that the drop is not the entire ocean. It could be said that the God Within is the drop of the ocean and the God Without is the ocean. Maybe?

"We are born to manifest the glory of God within us, it is in everyone . . . And as we let our light shine, we unconsciously give people permission to do the same." Marianne Williamson

"I am a candle lit by another candle." Rabbi Akiva

"The image of the morning sun in a dew drop is not less than the sun. The reflection of life in your soul is not less than life." Gibran

"What shall I say of him who is the pursuer playing the part of the pursued?" Gibran

And from the dictionary, na·ma·ste:

Noun—a conventional Hindu expression on meeting or parting, used by the speaker usually while holding the palms together vertically in front of the bosom.

Namaste—I honor the place in you in which the entire universe dwells. I honor the place in you which is love, truth, light and peace.

Amen

Meditation

This is a time to go within and be with your God. Your God in whatever form that brings love, light and peace to your soul. The God who created the heavens, the earth and all beauty there of. The God who created you and the goodness of that God dwells in you.

Honor the place in you in which the entire universe dwells. Honor that place in all others. We are one in love. One in God, One in the I AM that lives within our being.

May our prayers for peace begin within and be heard in the heavens and on earth, in the hearts of all.

And so it is!

Notes

All Bible references are from the King James Version, Nelson edition unless otherwise noted.

Photograph by Nancy Plantinga

Section 1

Don Miguel Ruiz, *The Four Agreements*

Matthew Kelly, *The Rhythm of Life*

Erma Bombeck, Article: *If I had to do My Life Over*

Edmund Rostand, *The Chanticleer*

The Oprah Show, May 25, 2011

Dr. Jill Bolt Taylor, *My Stroke of Insight*

Section 2

David Richo, *How to be an Adult in Relationships*

David Richo, *Daring to Trust*

Iyanla Vanzant, *Until Today*

Perma Chodron, *Taking the Leap*

Mary Anne Radmacher in *Courage Doesn't Always Roar*

Dr. Victor Frankl, *Man's Search for Meaning*

Byron Katie, *Loving What Is!*

Jack Canfield, *The Chicken Soup Series for the Soul*

Eckhart Tolle, *The New Earth*

A Course in Miracles

Don Miguel Ruiz, *Mastery of Love*

Section 3

Paulo Coelho, *The Alchemist*

Paulo Coelho, *Warrior of Light*

Section 4

A Course in Miracles

Don Miguel Ruiz, *Mastery of Love*

N. Douglas Walsh, *Conversations with God*

Dr. Bruce Lipton, *The Biology of Belief*

Louise Hay, *Heal Your Body, Heal Your Life*

Dr. C. Norman Shealy, *Energy of Medicine*

Norman Cousins, *The Anatomy of an Illness*

Maria Nemeth, *The Energy of Money*

Dr. Jill Bolt Taylor, *My Stroke of Insight*

Section 5

A Course in Miracles

Science of Mind

Don Miguel Ruiz, *The Four Agreements*

N. Douglas Walsh, *Conversations with God*

Touber, *A Crash Course in Enlightenment*

Jean Borysenko, *FRIED, Why You Burn Out and How to Revive*

Section 6

Rainer Maria Rilke, *Letters to a Young Poet*

Science of Mind

Victor Frankl, *Man's Search for Meaning*

The Story of the Monk and Farmer comes from Russell Conwell, founder and first president of Temple University in Philadelphia, Pennsylvania, (Feb 15, 1843-Dec 6, 1925).

Robert Heinlein, *Between Planets*

Catherine Ryan Hyde, *Pay It Forward*

Thich Nhat Hanh, *The Heart of the Buddha*

Section 8

Julia Duin, http://www.juliaduin.com/articles/

Dr. Rodney Stark (Baylor University Press, 2008), *What Americans Really Believe*

Michael Beckwith, *Spiritual Liberation*

Three Books of Enoch

Doreen Virtue, *Earth Angels*

Doreen Virtue, *How to Hear Your Angels*

Section 9

Don Miguel Ruiz, *The Four Agreements*

William P. Young, *The Shack*

Esther and Jerry Hicks, *Ask and it is Given*

Rainer Maria Rilke, *Letters to a Young Poet*

CPSIA information can be obtained at www.ICGtesting.com
Printed in the USA
BVOW082152090613

322751BV00002B/2/P